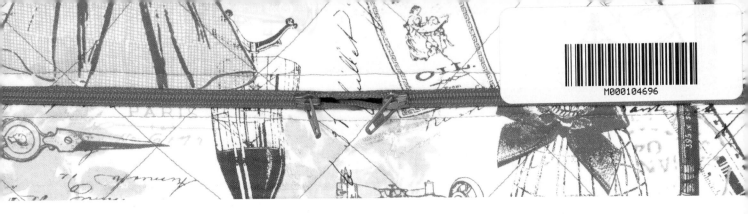

Sew Very Easy
Patternless Sewing Laura Coia

23 Skill-Building Projects
Bags, Accessories, Home Decor, Gifts & More

C&T PUBLISHING

Photography copyright © 2022 by Laura Coia

Text, photography, and artwork © 2022 by C&T Publishing, Inc.

Publisher: Amy Barrett-Daffin

Creative Director: Gailen Runge

Acquisitions Editor: Roxane Cerda

Managing Editor: Liz Aneloski

Editors: Liz Aneloski, Kristyne Czepuryk, and Karla Menaugh

Technical Editor: Debbie Rodgers

Cover/Book Designer: April Mostek

Production Coordinators: Tim Manibusan and Zinnia Heinzmann

Production Editor: Jennifer Warren

Photography Assistant: Gabriel Martinez

Models: Elisa Herberg (pages 2, 7, 9, 14, 19, 23, 58, 61, 76, and 90) and Yen Nguyen (pages 15, 17, 20, 24, 27, and 52)

Cover photography by Ivo Coia

Instructional photography by Laura Coia; lifestyle and subjects photography by Lauren Herberg of C&T Publishing, Inc.

Published by C&T Publishing, Inc., P.O. Box 1456, Lafayette, CA 94549

Library of Congress Cataloging-in-Publication Data

Names: Coia, Laura Ann, 1959- author.

Title: Sew very easy patternless sewing : 23 skill-building projects; bags, accessories, home decor, gifts & more / Laura Coia.

Description: Lafayette, CA : C&T Publishing, [2022]

Identifiers: LCCN 2021032257 | ISBN 9781644031261 (trade paperback) | ISBN 9781644031278 (ebook)

Subjects: LCSH: Sewing. | Textile crafts. | Tote bags. | House furnishings.

Classification: LCC TT705 .C723 2022 | DDC 646/1--dc23

LC record available at https://lccn.loc.gov/2021032257

Printed in the USA

10 9 8 7 6 5 4 3 2 1

Dedication

A very special thank you to all of my wonderful YouTube friends. Your heartfelt comments, love, and support keep me going. I get up every morning excited and inspired to find new ideas and projects that I can share with you, which in turn also makes me very happy. I thank *you*, from the bottom of my heart.

Acknowledgments

I do not think there is enough paper space for me to acknowledge everyone who deserves acknowledgment. So many of my YouTube family and friends have been constantly encouraging me to write this book on patternless sewing—so thank you for that.

Thank you, C&T Publishing, for all your help. You have been absolutely amazing to work with. I truly mean that.

To my mother, who taught me to sew and create by remaking, reusing, and recreating. She showed me by example that it is a greater gift to give than to receive. For that, I will always be thankful.

Many thanks to my children, which include my daughter-in-law, sons-in-law, and my grandchildren; *they inspire me*. They believe that I can make anything. They never laugh at the crazy things that I want to make, and oftentimes, they help me think of crazy things to make!

My extended family and friends, who let me babble on with excitement about new and fun projects: I do not know how you put up with me sometimes! Thank you for all your love and support.

However, my biggest thank you goes to my husband, Ivo. You have been my rock, my timekeeper, time-saver, pusher, and puller of all things that I need. It was 52 years ago that we met, and I would never take back a single moment. You make me believe, let me fly, and help me reach goals that sometimes I didn't even know that I had. To say that I love you doesn't ever seem like enough, but I do. LLAC

Contents

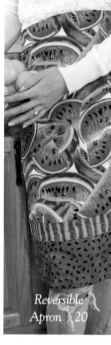

For the Home   52

Sewing Accessories   67

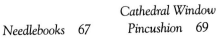

Introduction

Patternless sewing is a fun way to sew and make wonderful projects. Start with simple shapes such as squares, rectangles, or circles. What size do these shapes have to be, you ask? Well, most times, that will be entirely up to you. The beauty is that you can use any fabric you already have that is cut into these shapes—or you can make these shapes from scratch. Basically, *you* are the designer of these projects.

If you want to make a big project, then just start with big shapes. For smaller projects, use smaller shapes. This is an ideal time to use up any of your fabric that may otherwise end up in the scrap basket. In fact, better yet, you can make these projects from fabric currently in your scrap basket. What a fantastic way to use up all of our beautiful fabrics!

These projects can be made quickly and easily as well, even while you have other projects on the go. Before you know it, you will have made a nice selection of items that you can use yourself or give away as gifts. It's always great to have a selection of items readily available—very handy for gift giving!

You will be able to custom-make some projects to fit your own needs or preferences. For example, you can make a sewing machine cover to fit the exact size of your particular machine. With the step-by-step plans included in this book, not only will it be easy for you to make a cover for your sewing machine but also for your serger and anything else … even covers for your coffee makers, blenders, or other small appliances.

Regardless of your sewing skill, you will be able to make these fun projects. Whether they are tiny, small, large, or huge—you will be able to make them all!

At the end of the day, the most important thing is to make sure you have fun and to make every day a "sewtacular" day!

Small Tissue Cover

FINISHED SIZE:
3½″ wide × 5″ high × ¼″ deep

This little travel tissue cover is so quick and fun to make. You can make it with or without a metal clasp. Once you've made one for yourself, you'll want to make more for all your family and friends.

Use Up Scraps

Requirements

Fabric: 1 rectangle 5½″ × 12½″

Fabric pen

Stiletto

½″-wide ribbon:
3″ length (*optional*)

½″ clasp (*optional*)

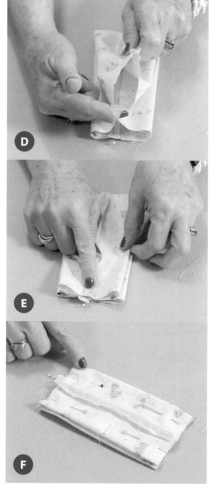

Construction

All seam allowances are ¼″ unless otherwise noted.

1. Fold the fabric right sides together to measure 5½″ × 6¼″. Sew along the 5½″ edge, leaving a 1½″ opening in the middle. Backstitch at both ends of the opening. Finger-press the seam open. *Fig. A*

2. Locate the center of each 6″ side between the fold and the seam. With a fabric pen, draw a 1″ line perpendicular to the fabric edge. Stitch along each pen mark, backstitching at both ends of each seam. *Fig. B*

3. *Optional:* To add a ribbon with a clasp, thread the ribbon through the clasp ring, fold the ribbon in half, and baste the ends of the ribbon together. Insert the ribbon/clasp inside the fabric close to the fold, placing the raw edges of the ribbon slightly above the edge of the fabric. Pin in place. *Fig. C*

4. At each end, align the fold, the 1″ seam, and the first seam, creating 2 folds on each side. Pin the layers together along both edges. *Figs. D–F*

5. Sew across both ends, starting and ending the seams with a backstitch. Backstitch to secure the ribbon. Trim the corners and excess ribbon. *Fig. G*

Align fold, 1″ seam, and first seam.

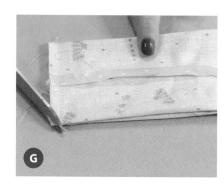

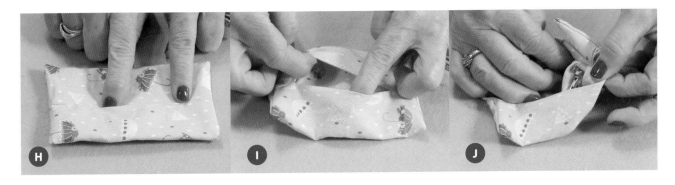

6. Turn to place the fabric right side out, but with the ribbon still on the inside. There will be a 1½″ opening on the bottom (used for turning) and a 3½″ tissue slot on the top. Shape all 4 corners. *Figs. H–J*

7. Whipstitch the 1½″ opening closed. *Fig. K*

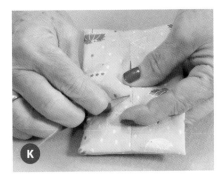

8. *Optional:* To square the corners, align a side seam with a side fold. Stitch across the corner, ¼″ from the tip. Repeat for all corners. Make sure the ribbon/clasp does not get caught in any seams. *Figs. L–M*

9. Finish turning right side out to bring the ribbon to the outside. Press if necessary. Insert tissue package. The initial fit will be very snug to ensure the tissues stay in place as they are removed. *Fig. N*

Eyeglass Case

FINISHED SIZE: 4¾″ × 9½″

I know we can buy cases for our glasses, but there is something fun about making one the size we want with the fabric we love. This case includes a practical surprise inside—a built-in cleaning cloth! It's sewn into the lining so it will always be handy and available whenever you need it.

Use Up Scraps

Sizeable

Requirements

Main fabric: 1 square 12″ × 12″

Lining fabric: 1 square 12″ × 12″

Sewable foam: 1 square 9½″ × 9½″ (I like ByAnnie's Soft and Stable.)

Cord: 16″ length for drawstring

Toggles or drawstring stoppers

Pencil and ruler

Large safety pin or flexible bodkin

Clear adhesive tape

Eyeglass cleaning cloth (optional)

Construction

All seam allowances are ¼″ unless otherwise noted.

1. Draw quilting lines on one side of the foam. With the marked side up, center the foam on the wrong side of the main fabric. Quilt the 2 layers together, following the drawn lines. *Fig. A*

2. Layer the quilted fabric square onto the lining, right sides together. Sew the fabric layers together along the top edge of the foam, using the foam edge as your sewing guide. Stitch from fabric edge to fabric edge. *Fig. B*

3. Mark ¼″ down from both top edges of the foam square. Repeat ¾″ from the top edges and again 1″ from the top edges. *Figs. C–D*

Mark ¼″, ¾″, and 1″.

4. Using the marks as a sewing guide, stitch along a side edge of the foam from the top edge to the ¼″ mark, starting and stopping with a few reverse stitches. Repeat between the ¾″ mark and the 1″ mark, leaving a gap to form the opening for the drawstring. Do the same to the opposite edge of the foam square. *Figs. E–F*

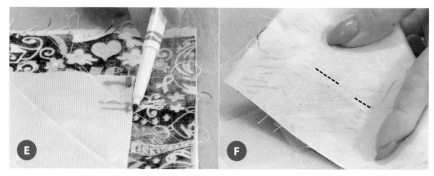

Stitch between ¼″ marks, leaving ½″ gap.

5. Trim the fabric, leaving a ¼″ seam allowance around the foam square. *Fig. G*

6. Open the case with both fabrics right side up. Lay the lining to one side and the quilted body to the other side. The 1″ stitched portion from the previous step will naturally lay under the lining. Fold the case in half, right sides together, aligning the folded seam. *Figs. H–I*

7. Stitch the quilted side of the case from the 1″ seam mark, down the side of the foam square, pivoting at the corner, and continuing along the bottom edge of the foam to the folded edge. Backstitch at the fold.

8. Fold the 1″ portion at the top of the case to the quilted body. Stitch the lining edges together from the 1″ mark down the side only. Leave the bottom edge of the lining open. *Figs. J–K*

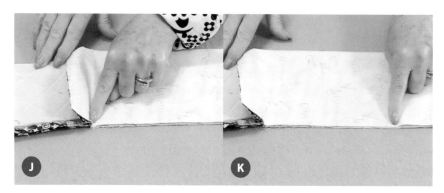

9. Trim the 4 corners of the seam allowance on the quilted body. *Fig. L*

10. Turn the case right side out, including the top flaps, and shape all the corners. *Fig. M*

11. Fold the raw edges of the lining ¼" to the wrong side and press.

12. *Optional:* Insert one corner of a cleaning cloth into the seam allowance. Pin and sew the opening closed, catching the cleaning cloth in the seam. *Fig. N*

13. Insert the lining into the case. Ensure the lining is smooth and even along the top edge. Pin and sew a row of stitching ¼" from the top edge of the case and a second row 1" from the top edge to create the drawstring channel. *Fig. O*

14. Use a safety pin or flexible bodkin to thread the drawstring through the channel. Thread both ends of the drawstring onto the toggle. *Fig. P*

Laura's Tip

Tape the ends of the drawstring like a shoelace to make them easier to thread into the toggle.

15. Knot the ends of the drawstring together to keep the toggle from slipping off. Trim and fray the ends of the drawstring. *Fig. Q*

Form drawstring channel with 2 rows of stitching.

Sew Very Easy Patternless Sewing

Hair Scrunchie

Like most of my "patterns," this project does not require 100 percent accuracy. The cutting dimensions are approximate. Small variances in the fabric will not affect the finish.

The elastic length can be cut longer or shorter, depending on the stretch of the elastic, the fabric thickness (velvet versus silk), and hair thickness.

Use Up Scraps
Sizeable
Use Reclaimed Fabrics

Construction

All seam allowances are ¼″ unless otherwise noted.

1. Press and fold the fat quarter in half, right sides together, twice to measure approximately 4½″ × 21″. Press the folds and trim the selvage. *Fig. A*

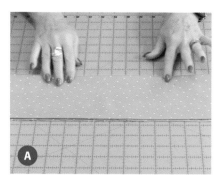

2. Open the fat quarter and cut along the folds to make 4 strips 21″ in length. *Fig. B*

3. Cut an 8″ length of elastic. Center it on the wrong side of a fabric strip. Sew one end of the elastic to a short edge of the fabric and secure with a few backstitches. Repeat with the opposite end. *Fig. C*

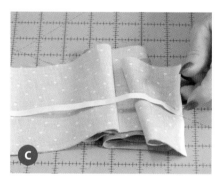

4. Ignoring the elastic, fold the fabric strip lengthwise, right sides together. Sew along the length to form a tube, starting and stopping the seam 2″ from each end. *Figs. D–E*

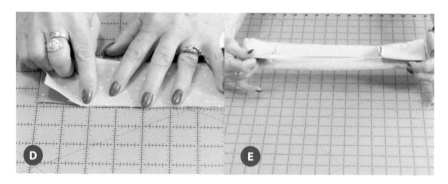

5. Turn the tube right side out. Flatten the elastic inside the tube at each end and pin in place. *Fig. F*

6. Pin and sew the short ends of the fabric right sides together. The elastic ends do not have to be aligned. Remove all pins. *Fig. G*

7. Tug the elastic to distribute the fabric evenly around the elastic. Tuck the seam allowances into the opening, pin, and machine or hand stitch the opening closed. *Fig. H*

8. Test the scrunchie and adjust the elastic length if necessary.

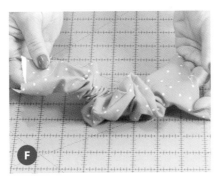

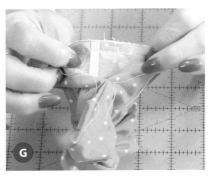

Measuring Tape Wristband

FINISHED SIZE: 1″ × 7″

When you need your hands free, this wristband can be so, well ... handy! Use the clip on the end to hold keys, a wallet, an ID tag, or anything you want to keep handy. You can easily adjust the length of the wristband or lanyard, depending on its use. The 16″ cut length in the pattern is for a large wrist.

Use Up Scraps
Sizeable
Use Reclaimed
Fabrics

Requirements

Fabric: 1 rectangle 2″ × 16″

Heavy fusible interfacing:
Create-a-Strap interfacing by
Clover, 1″ size (A package yields
approximately 5 wristbands.)

Swivel hook with 1″ ring

Plastic measuring tape:
Less than 1″ wide with metal
ends trimmed off

**Strong, sharp sewing machine
needle (Microtex)**

Large fabric clips

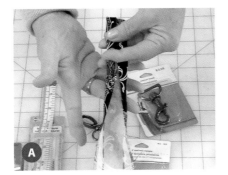

Fold raw edges to center.

Construction

1. Cut a 16″ strip from the Create-a-Strap interfacing. Following the manufacturer's instructions, fuse the interfacing strip to the wrong side of the fabric strip. Fold the long edges, wrong sides together, along the precut slots. Press. *Fig. A*

2. Cut a 16″ length from the tape measure. Center it on the strap, covering the raw edges of the fabric. Using fabric clips to hold the tape measure in place, sew both edges of the tape measure to the wristband with a scant ⅛″ topstitch. *Figs. B–C*

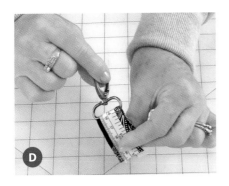

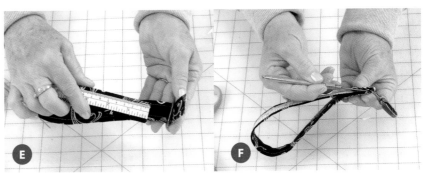

Nest both raw edges at fold.

3. Fold the strap 2″ from one end, wrong sides together. Thread the strap through the clasp ring and position the ring at the fold. *Fig. D*

4. Insert the other end of the strap under the 2″ fold so the raw edge meets the fold. Then tuck the 2″ section under itself so both raw edges meet at the fold. *Figs. E–F*

5. Starting at the centerline of the measuring tape, sew a rectangle at the fold to secure the ring in place. *Fig. G*

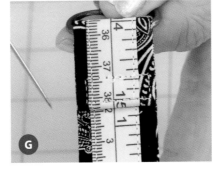

Reversible Apron

FINISHED SIZE: 17″ × 22″

Whether you're hosting a dinner party, working in the garden, doing house chores, or painting in your studio, protect your outfit with a pretty and practical apron. Have some fun with your fabric stash and choose prints to suit the chore or the occasion.

Requirements

Main fabric: ½ yard

Trim fabric: 1 strip 2″ × width of fabric

Border fabric: 1 strip 4½″ × width of fabric

Tie fabric: 2 strips 6½″ × width of fabric

Temporary fabric pen

Construction

All seam allowances are ¼″ unless otherwise noted.

1. Sew the 2″ trim to the bottom edge of the main fabric. Then sew the 4½″ border to the trim. Do not press. Right sides together, fold the trim and border fabric onto the main fabric. Trim both sides to straighten; remove selvages if necessary. *Figs. A–B*

2. Fold the panel in half, right sides together, and align the trimmed sides. Finger-press the fold to mark the center. Cut the panel in half along the center fold. *Fig. C*

3. Press the seam allowances up on one half and down on the other half so they lie in opposite directions. Topstitch all seam allowances ¼″ from the edge. *Fig. D*

4. On each side of one panel, fold the fabric to the wrong side ¼″; then fold again ¼″ to create a double-fold ¼″ hem. Press and topstitch the hems in place, close to the inside edge. Repeat for the other panel. *Fig. E*

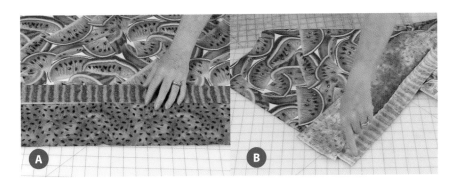

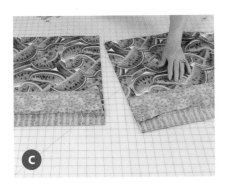

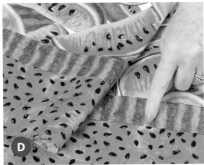

Topstitch seam allowances.

5. Lay both panels right sides together, aligning the trim and border seams. (The seam allowances that were pressed in opposite directions will nest nicely at the edges.) Sew them together along the top and bottom edges. Turn the panel right side out. Press the top and bottom seams flat. Then topstitch the pressed seams ¼″ from the edge. *Fig. F*

6. Measure 3½″ down from the top edge of the apron. Draw a line across the apron and sew a seam along the line, sewing both layers together. *Fig. G*

7. From a top corner of the apron, measure down 5½″ and mark with a pin. Repeat on the opposite side. Measure and place another pin down 12½″ from the top corner on both sides. *Figs. H–I*

Sew both layers of a side together between the 3½″ and 5½″ marks. Then stitch both layers together from the 12½″ mark to the bottom edge. Repeat on the opposite side. *Figs. J–K*

8. Right sides together, sew the 6½″ tie fabric strips together with a ½″ seam to make a long tie measuring approximately 84″. Press the seam open. Fold the tie in half lengthwise, right sides together. Sew the raw edges together, leaving a 4″ opening near the middle seam for turning. To form a point on each end of the tie, pivot 2″ from the end and sew diagonally to the fold. Trim the corners. *Figs. L–M*

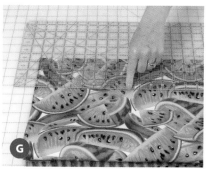

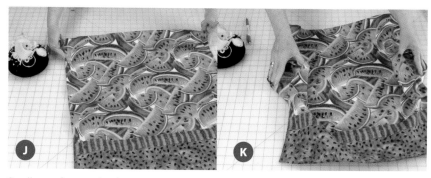

Small gaps form casing for apron ties.

Large gaps form pocket openings to bottom of apron.

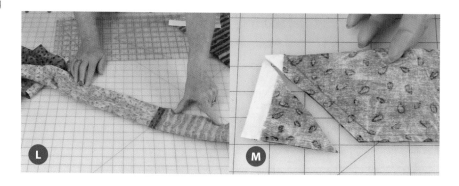

9. Turn the tie right side out and shape the points. Tuck the opening seam allowances inside and press. Topstitch around all edges.

10. Insert the tie into the 3½″ channel at the top of the apron.

Laura's Tip

To insert the tie into the channel easily, fold one end of the tie over a 12″ ruler and secure the tie to the ruler with a binder clip. Fold the clip handles down flat. Insert the ruler into the channel, binder first, until the clip appears at the opposite end.

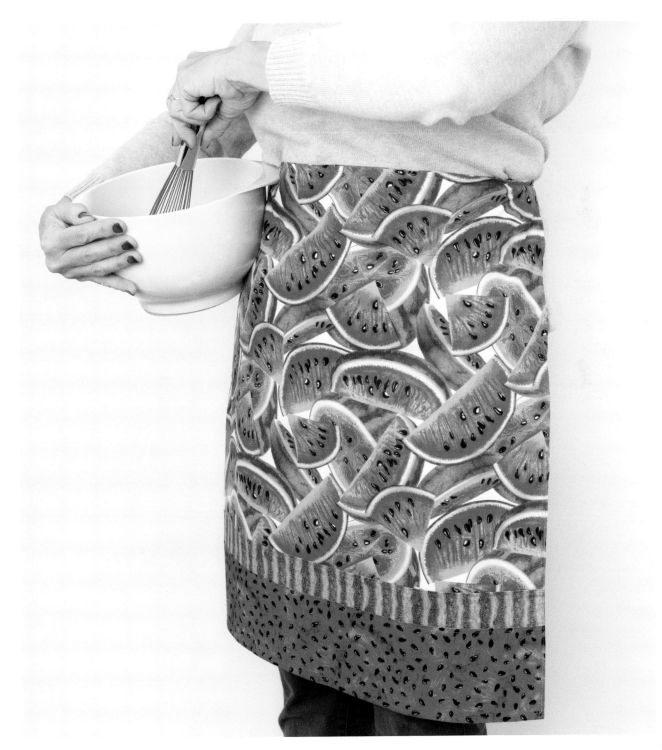

Scrub Cap

Scrub caps aren't just for medical workers. We can use them to protect our hair and keep it off our face during messy tasks like painting or yard work. And they also come in handy when we're having a bad hair day!

Precut Friendly

Requirements

Main fabric: 2 fat quarters

Coordinating tie fabric: 2 strips 2½″ × 22″

¼″ elastic: 8″ length

Erasable fabric pen, such as a FriXion pen (by Pilot)

Flexible bodkin or large safety pin

Construction

All seam allowances are ¼″ unless otherwise noted.

1. Fold a 2½″ × 22″ strip in half lengthwise, right sides together. Starting with a backstitch, sew across one short end and down the length, leaving the other short end open. Trim the corner at the stitched short end. Turn the fabric tube right side out. Shape the corners and press. Repeat to make the second tie. *Figs. A–B*

2. Insert ½″ of the elastic into the opening of one tie and sew in place. Repeat with the other tie. *Fig. C*

3. Press both fat quarters and lay them right sides together. Trim to straighten all 4 edges. *Fig. D*

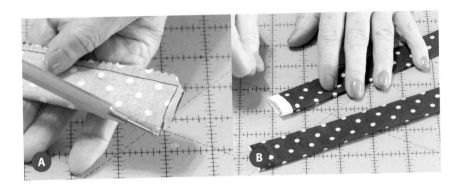

4. Starting 1″ from the short side, sew about 4″ along a long edge, backstitching at both ends. This seam will form the edge that will lay along the forehead. Leave a 5″ space, then sew the rest of the long side together, stopping 1″ from the other short side. Backstitch at both ends of the seam. *Figs. E–G*

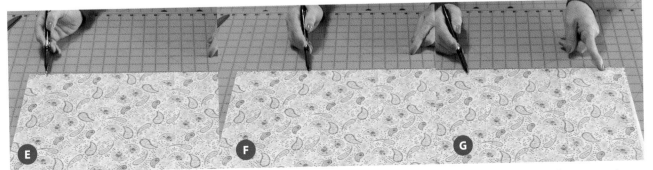

Measure 1″ from edge.

Sew 4″ from 1″ mark.

Measure 5″ from end of first seam and sew rest of length, leaving 1″ unstitched at other end.

5. Keeping both fabric layers together, fold them in half to measure approximately 11″ × 18″. Starting 7″ from the bottom edge, cut a gentle curve across the bottom corner through all layers. It does not have to be accurate. *Fig. H*

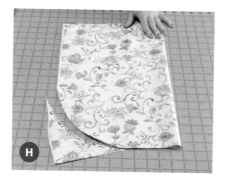

6. Unfold the layers. Sew the remaining 3 sides together, starting and stopping at the top edge. Press the seams. *Fig. I*

7. Turn the cap right side out. Tuck the opening allowances inside and press. Ignore the corner openings for now. *Fig. J*

8. To form the casing for the ties, start at a top edge and sew a ¾″ seam from the edge along the 3 curved sides. Backstitch at both ends. *Fig. K*

9. Using a bodkin or safety pin, insert the tie through the entire length of the casing. Pull the ties out on either side with just the elastic in the casing. Insert the seam allowance of one tie into the casing opening. Pin in place. Repeat with the other tie. *Figs. L–M*

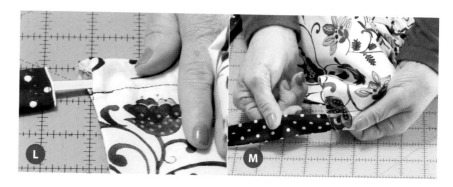

10. Topstitch ⅛″ from the top edge, starting and ending with backstitching to secure the ties into the casing opening. This will also close the opening you left in the top center for turning. *Fig. N*

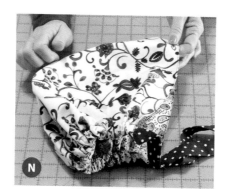

Little Drawstring Bag

FINISHED SIZE:
6″ wide × 5″ high × 6″ deep

I made this drawstring bag using precut fabric because, well ... they're already cut for me! But you can use any size of square you like, just as long as they're all the same size. This may seem strange, but it really is "sew very easy."

Use Up Scraps
Sizeable
Precut Friendly

Requirements

Assorted fabrics: 12 charm squares (5″ × 5″)

Drawstring cord: 2 lengths, 30″ each

Fabric glue stick

Flexible bodkin or safety pin

Construction

All seam allowances are ¼″ unless otherwise noted.

1. Select 4 squares for the drawstring casing.

2. On the wrong side of a casing square, apply glue to 2 opposite corners. Fold each corner over, wrong sides together. The folded triangle should measure approximately 1″. *Fig. A*

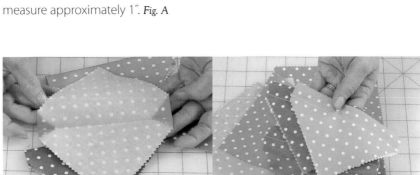

Fold the square in half diagonally, wrong sides together, across the glued corners. Press. Sew a ¾″ seam along the folded edge. Make 4 casing triangles. *Figs. B–C*

3. Sew the remaining 8 squares in pairs to make 4 sets. *Fig. D*

4. Right sides together, lay a casing square onto a sewn pair, aligning the straight (left) edges. Pin in place. *Fig. E*

5. Glue and fold under the corner of the top square to match the casing triangle's folded corner. *Fig. F*

6. Sew the casing triangle to the squares across the top edge, backstitching at the folded corner. Make 4 units. *Fig. G*

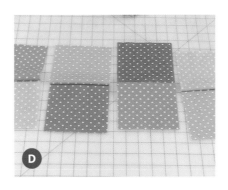

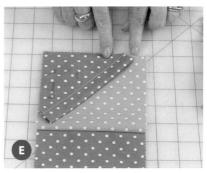

7. Rotate a unit 90°. Align the bottom edge of the unit to the left side of a bottom square of another unit. Sew them right sides together along the bottom edge of the top unit. Make 2 L units. *Figs. H–I*

8. Lay both L units right sides up to form a pinwheel. *Fig. J*

9. Flip the bottom L onto the top L, right sides together. Sew the units together along the middle 2 squares. Press all seams flat. *Fig. K*

10. Fold the pinwheel shape, aligning 2 adjoining sides right sides together. *Fig. L*

Line up the casing folded corners and seams, and pull the bottom out of the way; then pin and sew the sides together, backstitching at both ends of the seam. *Fig. M*

Repeat for all sides. *Fig. N*

11. Using a safety pin or flexible bodkin, thread the drawstring through all 4 casing sections. *Fig. O*

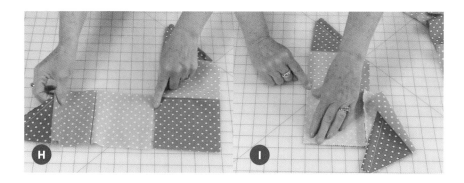

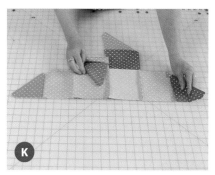

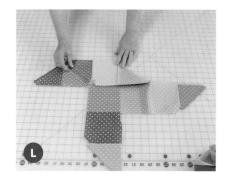
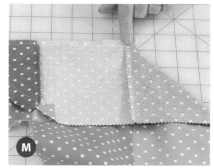

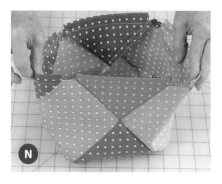
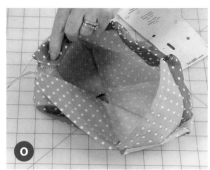

12. Tie the drawstring ends together, leaving a few inches of cord beyond the casing. Trim excess string. Add a second drawstring in the opposite direction, if desired. *Figs. P–Q*

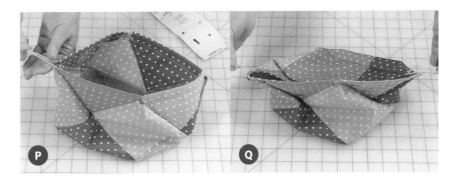

Triangle Bag

FINISHED SIZE: 6½″ wide × 6½″ high × 6½″ deep

I always rescue perfectly good zippers and sections of fabric before discarding worn out garments. Salvaged zippers and denim are perfect for this little project. The finished size of this bag is dictated by the length of the zipper. These instructions are written for a 5″ zipper. But you can use any length of zipper you want—you just need to adjust the size of the fabric squares. The rule of thumb is to cut the body and lining squares 2″ bigger than the finished length of the zipper. For example, if the finished zipper length is 8″, cut the body and lining squares 10″ × 10″.

Use Up Scraps
Sizeable
Use Reclaimed Fabrics

Requirements

Body fabric: 2 squares 7˝ × 7˝

Lining fabric (lightweight recommended): 4 zipper end squares 3˝ × 3˝ and 2 lining squares 7˝ × 7˝

Light- or midweight fusible interfacing: 2 squares 7˝ × 7˝

5˝ zipper

Decorative trim, embroidery, beads, or other embellishment (optional)

Laura's Note

Any zipper will work for this project. Just be aware that zippers with metal teeth are difficult to adjust in length, and they cannot be run over with a machine needle. Zippers with plastic teeth can be trimmed to any size, and you can easily stitch over the teeth with a sewing machine.

Construction

All seam allowances are ¼˝ unless otherwise noted.

1. Lay the closed end of the zipper onto a zipper end square, right sides together, aligning the raw edges at the center of the fabric edge. Pin in place. Keeping the zipper visible at the sewing machine, sew across the zipper a scant ⅛˝ from the metal stop at the end of the teeth. Take care to avoid running over the metal with your needle! *Fig. A*

2. Lay another zipper end square to the same end of the zipper, right sides together. With the seam from Step 1 visible, sew the 3 layers together exactly along the seam. Fold and press both squares away from the zipper. *Optional:* Sew a row of topstitching along the seam. *Figs. B–C*

3. Repeat with the remaining zipper end squares on the other end of the zipper. Open the zipper a few inches to ensure the tab is out of the way, and pin the zipper end to the square so both halves of the zipper meet. *Figs. D–E*

4. Fuse the interfacing squares to the wrong side of the main fabric squares.

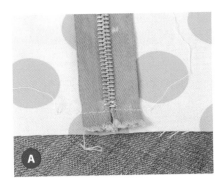

5. *Optional:* Embellish the right side of one or both body squares with decorative trim, embroidery, beads, and so on. *Fig. F*

6. Lay the zipper along one edge of a body square, right sides together, ensuring the ends of the zipper meet the edges of the square. *Fig. G*

7. With the zipper foot installed on your sewing machine, sew the zipper to the body with an ⅛″ seam. Trim the zipper end squares even with the seam allowance. *Fig. H*

8. Repeat to add the second body square to the zipper. *Fig. I*

9. Align the right side of a lining square edge with the wrong side of one zipper edge. Sew the lining to the zipper/body with a ¼″ seam. *Figs. J–K*

Repeat to add the other lining square. *Figs. L–M*

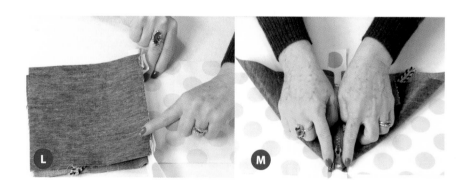

10. Trim the zipper end squares. *Fig. N*

11. *Optional:* Add topstitching along both sides of the zipper, keeping the lining free. *Fig. O*

12. Open the zipper halfway. Lay the body squares right sides together and the lining squares right sides together. Fold the zipper ends toward the lining, match up the seams, and pin in place. Align and sew the long edges. *Figs. P–Q*

13. Open the zipper all the way. Fold the body squares in half to align the side seams. Pin the seam allowances in opposite directions. *Fig. R*

Sew a seam along the edge, backstitching at both ends. Trim the corners. *Fig. S*

14. Repeat with the lining, leaving at least a 2″ opening for turning. *Fig. T*

Laura's Note

If your bag is very small, it may be better to leave the entire end open and stitch it closed after the bag is turned right side out.

15. Turn the bag right side out and shape the corners. Tuck the opening seam allowance inside and stitch it closed.

Fold zipper end toward lining.

Sew long edges.

Reversible Storage Bag

These storage or gift bags are a great way to use up leftover fabrics and put a little dent in your scrap pile. Make the outside of the bag with a single piece of fabric, or piece some scraps together for a fun patchwork finish. And you can make this bag any size you want! The measurements in this pattern yield a 14½″ × 16″ bag, but you can cut your body and lining rectangles to any size you like. A little bonus—this bag is totally reversible!

*Use Up Scraps
Sizeable*

Requirements

Body fabric: 1 rectangle 15″ × 33″ (pieced or wholecloth)

Lining fabric: 1 rectangle 15″ × 33″

Drawstring: 2 lengths, 38″ each

Flexible bodkin or safety pin

Fabric glue *(optional)*

Construction

All seam allowances are ¼″ unless otherwise noted.

1. Lay the body and lining rectangles right sides together. Sew the layers together along both short sides. *Fig. A*

2. Align the side seams right sides together. Press the seam allowances in opposite directions. *Fig. B*

3. Mark 1″ and 2″ from the seam on both sides. Repeat on the opposite edge. The spaces between the 1″ and 2″ marks will form the drawstring casing. *Fig. C*

Laura's Note

For a larger bag, you can increase the first mark to 2″ and the second mark to 4″. For a smaller bag, decrease the first mark to ½″ and the second mark to 1″.

4. Sew the long sides of the bag, leaving the drawstring casing space unstitched. Backstitch on both sides of the openings. Leave a 3″ opening along one side of the lining for turning. *Fig. D*

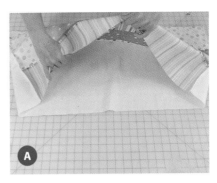

A

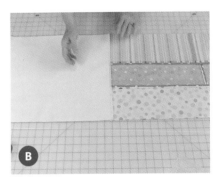

B

C

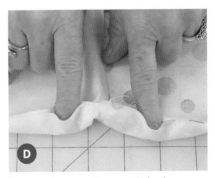

D

Leave casing openings unstitched.

5. Fold all 8 seam allowances at the casing openings wrong sides together, and glue in place. *Figs. E–F*

6. With the bag still inside out, fold it in half along the center seam, aligning the lining and body corners. Then fold in half in the other direction, aligning all 4 corners. Cut out a 1″ square, going through all layers at once. *Fig. G*

Laura's Note

For larger bags, cut a 1½″ or 2″ square.
For smaller bags, cut a ½″ or ¾″ square.

7. At one corner, open out the sides of the corner square. Align the side seam with the bottom fold, pin, and sew across the corner. Repeat for all corners. *Fig. H*

8. Turn the bag right side out and shape the corners. Sew the opening in the lining closed. Insert the lining into the bag and match up the corners. Topstitch around the opening, ⅛″ from the top edge. Press the bag.

9. To complete the casing, mark lines 1″ and 2″ from the top of the bag. Stitch around the bag on both lines. *Fig. I*

10. Using a flexible bodkin or safety pin, thread the drawstring through the casing. *Fig. J*

11. Tie the drawstring ends together, leaving a few inches of cord beyond the casing. Trim the excess string. Add a second drawstring in the opposite direction. *Fig. K*

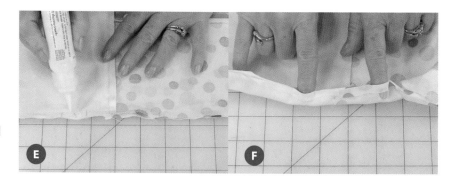

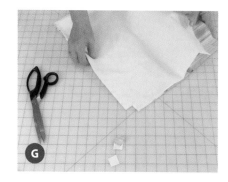

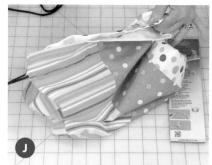

Strawberry Bag

FINISHED SIZE: Approximately 1½″ wide × 1½″ high × 1½″ deep

Sometimes you really want to make something, but you don't have a lot of spare time. This sweet strawberry bag is just the thing because it only takes a few minutes to complete, especially if you start with precut squares.

Use Up Scraps
Precut Friendly
Use Reclaimed Fabrics

Requirements

Main fabric: 1 square 5″ × 5″
(*Optional:* pinked edge)

Lining fabric: 1 square 5″ × 5″
(*Optional:* pinked edge)

Yarn: 2 lengths,
15″ each for drawstring

Large darning needle

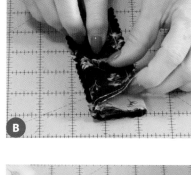

Construction

All seam allowances are ¼″ unless otherwise noted.

1. Lay both fabric squares wrong sides together. Stitch around all edges. *Fig. A*

2. Fold the sewn squares into thirds, with the main fabric facing up. *Fig. B*

3. With the main fabric on top, fold and pin both top corners right sides together to expose the lining. *Fig. C*

4. Flip the folded unit over. Fold and pin both corners with the body fabric right sides together. *Fig. D*

5. Open the trifolds. Sew across each folded edge, backstitching at both ends of each seam. *Fig. E*

6. Thread the yarn onto a darning needle. Insert the needle, eye end first, through all of the casing channels. Repeat to add a second drawstring that starts and ends on the opposite side. Tie the drawstring ends together close to the casing. Trim the excess yarn about 1½″ from the knots and fray the ends. *Figs. F–G*

7. Pull the drawstrings to shape the bag. *Fig. H*

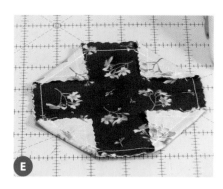

Insert eye end of needle first.

Fat Quarter-Friendly Drawstring Bag

FINISHED SIZE:
7½˝ wide × 8˝ high × 2˝ deep

This fun, quick, and easy bag is a great project because you never know when you're going to need a cute little gift to give. This fat quarter-friendly bag can be used as either the gift itself or perform double duty as the gift bag that will surely be used for other things by the recipient! Grab a big handful of fat quarters and make a bunch so you're always prepared to make someone smile.

Precut Friendly

Requirements

Body fabric: 1 square 17½″ × 17½″

Lining fabric: 1 square 17½″ × 17½″

Laura's Tip

I used a contrasting fabric for the lining, which will show on the front of the bag when you pull the drawstrings.

Ribbon: 2 lengths, 24″ each for drawstrings

Temporary fabric pen

Flexible bodkin or safety pin

Construction

All seam allowances are ¼″ unless otherwise noted.

1. Lay the fabric squares right sides together and stitch around all edges, leaving a 3″ opening in the middle of one edge. Trim the corners. *Fig. A*

Laura's Tip

Press the seam allowances over at the opening to make it easier to stitch closed when the bag is turned right side out.

2. Turn the bag right side out, shape the corners, and press the edges well. Topstitch around the square ⅛″ from the edge.

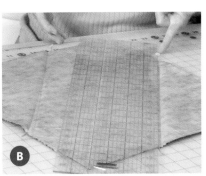

3. On the lining, draw a diagonal line from corner to corner. Measure 4″ from that centerline and mark that point with a pin on both edges. Repeat on the other side of the diagonal line. *Fig. B*

4. Fold a point onto the body, right sides of the lining together, at the pins. Fold the opposite point, right sides together, slightly overlapping the first point. These folded edges form the sides of the bag. *Fig. C*

5. Fold the remaining 2 points right sides together, almost meeting the edges of the first 2 points. Leave a small space between the edges so the lining is slightly visible. Press well. These shorter folded edges form the top edges of the bag. *Fig. D*

6. Topstitch ¼″ from the edge along one fold at the top edge of the bag. Topstitch a second row ¾″ from the edge. Backstitch at both ends of the seams. Repeat on the other top edge. *Fig. E*

7. Topstitch a line through the center of the bag from side fold to side fold. Backstitch at both ends of the seam. *Fig. F*

8. Fold the bag along the center stitched line with the points inside, aligning the top corners. Then sew both sides closed with a ⅛″ seam. *Fig. G*

9. To square the bottom corners, fold the bag to align the side seam with the bottom middle stitched line. Mark a line 1″ from the point and sew along that line. Repeat to form the other corner. *Figs. H–I*

10. Turn the bag right side out. Using a flexible bodkin or safety pin, thread the drawstring through the entire casing. Add a second drawstring in the opposite direction. Tie the drawstring ends together, leaving a few inches of ribbon beyond the casing. *Fig. J*

Contrast lining will show when you pull drawstrings.

Denim-Lined Sack

FINISHED SIZE: Approximately 4″ wide × 8″ high × 4″ deep

If you have a pair of worn-out jeans, you can learn how to turn each pant leg into a cute little sack. They're a lot of fun to make, and they each have their own personality, just like a well-loved pair of jeans.

This pattern uses a 10″-wide pant leg, but as with many of my projects, you can easily adjust the dimensions to accommodate your pant leg.

Sizeable
Use Reclaimed
Fabrics

Requirements

Pant leg: Approximately 15″ long, including the bottom hem

Lining fabric: 1 square 17½″ × 17½″

Mid- to heavyweight fusible interfacing, such as 809 Décor-Bond (by Pellon)

Tailor's chalk or other fabric marker

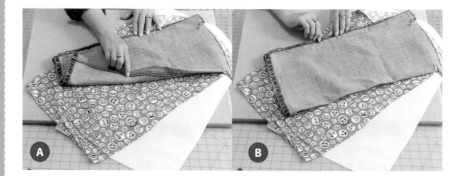

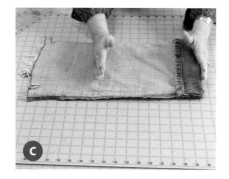

Construction

All seam allowances are ¼″ unless otherwise noted.

1. Most jean legs have 1 flatlock seam, where the seam allowance has been stitched down to the pant, and 1 free seam. Fold the leg along the free seam. Press. *Figs. A–B*

2. Fold the bottom hem, wrong sides together, to form a cuff approximately 2″–2½″ deep. *Fig. C*

3. Measure 8″ from the cuff fold and mark with a chalk line. *Fig. D*

4. Measure 10½″ from the cuff fold and mark another chalk line. Unfold the cuff. *Fig. E*

5. Fold the lining fabric in half. Align a raw edge of the lining fabric with the farthest chalk line and trim the lining to align with the hem of the jeans. *Fig. F*

6. Lay the interfacing on the wrong side of the lining, leaving a ¼″ seam allowance of the lining free along the top edge. Trim the other 3 sides of the interfacing to the same size as the lining. Fuse the interfacing to the wrong side of the lining. Fold and press the seam allowance at the top of the lining to the interfacing side. *Fig. G*

7. Fold the lining in half, right sides together, aligning the seam allowance edge.

8. Lay the pant leg on the folded lining, aligning both side folds. Align the inside edge of the pant hem with the top folded edge of the lining so the pant leg extends a little beyond the lining fold. *Fig. H*

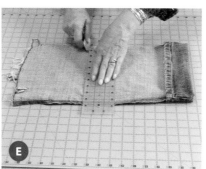

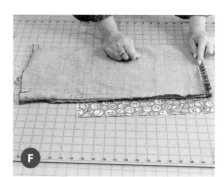

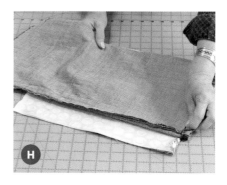

9. Fold the leg's free seam allowance up and trace the seamline onto the lining. *Fig. I*

10. Unfold the top seam allowance on the lining and stitch along the drawn seamline. Trim, leaving a 1″ seam allowance, and press open. Refold the top edge. Turn the lining right side out. *Fig. J*

11. Insert the pant leg into the lining, wrong sides together. Align the folded edge of the lining with the inside edge of the pant hem. Pin the layers together and topstitch close to the lining fold. *Figs. K–L*

12. Trim all layers even with the farthest marked line on the pant leg. *Fig. M*

13. Fold the bag in half, ensuring all layers are flat. Draw and cut out a 2″ square through all layers on both corners of the bottom edge. Turn the lining inside out. *Figs. N–O*

14. Sew across the bottom edge of the leg. *Fig. P*

Trim bottom edge.

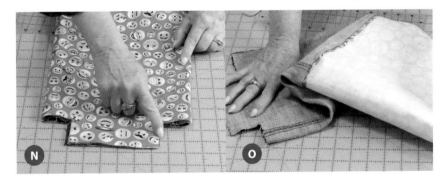

15. Align the side and bottom seams. Pin and sew across the opening. Repeat for the other corner. *Figs. Q–R*

16. Repeat Steps 14 and 15 to form the lining corners, leaving a 3″ opening along the bottom edge. *Fig. S*

17. Turn both the bag and lining right side out and shape the outside corners. Topstitch the opening in the lining closed. Insert the lining inside the bag and match up the corners. Fold the cuff to desired length.

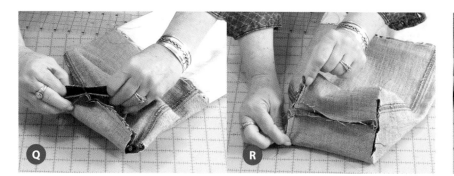

Easy Zipper Pouch

FINISHED SIZE:
3″ wide × 4″ high × 1½″ deep

Little zipper pouches are a lot of fun to make, and they're also a lot of fun to give. We can always find something to put inside them. They're also a great way to use up some leftover fabric.

Use Up Scraps
Sizeable
Use Reclaimed Fabrics

Easy Zipper Pouch   **49**

Requirements

Main fabric: 1 rectangle 5″ × 9″. Use a midweight, like a canvas. If you choose lightweight fabric, line it with fusible interfacing.

Contrast fabric: 1 rectangle 3¼″ × 6″

Plastic zipper: At least 5″ in length (will be trimmed)

Ribbon: 3″ length

Fabric glue

Construction

All seam allowances are ¼″ unless otherwise noted.

1. Zigzag the edges of the main fabric.

2. Apply glue to the right side of a 5″ edge of the fabric. Open the zipper. Lay it onto the glued fabric edge, right sides together, aligning the flat edge of the zipper tape with the edge of the fabric. Press to set the glue. Repeat on the other side. *Fig. A*

3. Using a zipper foot, sew each side of the zipper to the fabric, approximately ¼″ from the teeth. *Fig. B*

4. Fold the zipper seam allowance to the wrong side and topstitch ⅛″ from the fold. *Fig. C*

Laura's Tip

Optional: Choose a decorative stitch for the topstitching for a pretty detail! *Fig. D*

5. Turn the bag inside out with the zipper closed, and trim the bottom end of the zipper to align with the edge of the bag.

6. Fold the bag so the zipper is in the middle. Tuck one folded edge toward the zipper to form a 1″ pleat. Pin or clip in place. Repeat on the other folded edge. *Fig. E*

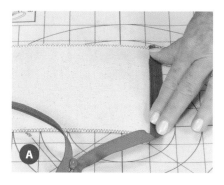

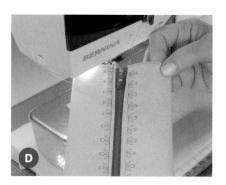

7. Sew the bottom edge of the bag closed with a ¼″ seam, backstitching at both ends of the seam.

8. Turn the bag right side out and shape the bottom corners. *Fig. F*

9. Repeat Step 6 to form pleats at the top edge of the bag, this time with the bag right side out. *Fig. G*

10. Pin the ends of the zipper so the halves meet, open the zipper, and sew the top edge closed with a scant ¼″ seam. *Fig. H*

11. Fold the ribbon in half and place it on the zipper (or anywhere along the top edge), aligning the raw edges with the top edge of the bag. *Fig. I*

12. Lay the contrast fabric on the front of the bag, right sides together. Fold the ends of the contrast fabric over the sides of the bag, and pin or clip in place. Don't worry if it won't meet at the back center. Restitch across the top edge of the bag with a full ¼″ seam. Fold the contrast fabric up so it is right side out. *Fig. J*

13. Fold the contrast band twice, wrong sides together, over the seam allowance to the back side, slightly covering the seam on the back. Pin or clip in place. *Fig. K*

14. Sew along the seam on the front, just catching the fold on the back. *Figs. L–M*

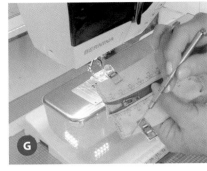

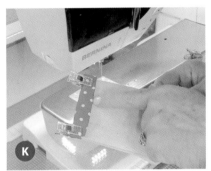

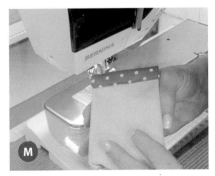

Hanging Door Pockets

FINISHED SIZE: 7″ × 10″

These quick and easy reversible bags fit perfectly onto a doorknob—a smart and convenient storage idea for your front door to keep your keys, wallet, and other little things that you don't want to lose.

Use Up Scraps

Requirements

The yardage yields 2 hanging pockets.

Main fabric: 1 square 16½˝ × 16½˝

Contrast fabric: 1 square 16½˝ × 16½˝

Mid- to heavyweight fusible interfacing: 2 squares 16˝ × 16˝ (I like 809 Décor-Bond by Pellon.)

Thread to match the main fabric for a buttonhole

Removable fabric pen, such as a FriXion pen (by Pilot)

Construction

All seam allowances are ¼˝ unless otherwise noted.

1. Cut both fabric squares and the interfacing square in half diagonally.

2. Trim each interfacing corner ½˝ from the point. *Fig. A*

3. Fuse an interfacing triangle on the wrong side of a fabric triangle, aligning the squared sides so the diagonal edge of the fabric has a seam allowance. Repeat with the contrast fabric triangle and remaining interfacing triangle. *Fig. B*

4. Layer the fused triangles right sides together. Sew the layers together around all 3 edges, leaving a 3˝ opening in the middle of the diagonal edge. Trim all corners. *Fig. C*

5. Along the 3˝ opening, press each seam allowance onto the interfacing. *Fig. D*

6. Turn the bag right side out, shape the corners, and press.

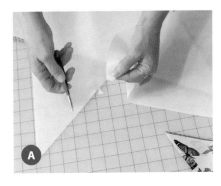

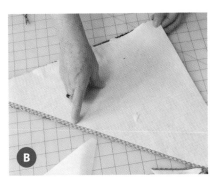

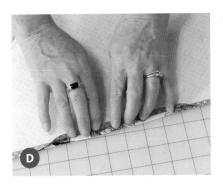

7. Starting ¾″ from the square corner, draw and sew a 2½″ buttonhole. Make a test buttonhole with scrap fabric to ensure it will fit over the desired door-knob and adjust as necessary. *Figs. E–F*

Laura's Tip

If your sewing machine does not allow for a buttonhole this long, sew a zigzag stitch down both sides of the drawn line and a few reinforcing stitches at both ends of the line.

8. Right sides together, fold the bag into thirds with both points meeting the side folds. *Figs. G–H*

9. Whipstitch all the layers together by hand along the bottom edge. *Fig. I*

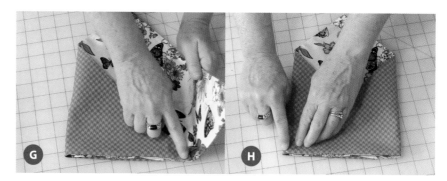

Hanging Open Storage

FINISHED SIZE:
11˝ wide × 21˝ high

Maximizing storage space in our home and sewing room is very important. Every space is definitely well worth using. Having an open storage bag leaves us with a lot of open opportunities to store.

Precut Friendly

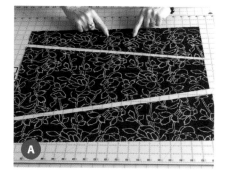

A

Construction

All seam allowances are ¼″ unless otherwise noted.

1. Lay both fat quarters right sides together, aligning all edges. Trim the edges so they are straight and they measure approximately 18½″ × 21½″. Keep the fabrics layered.

2. Mark the center of both short edges with pins. These pins are at the top and bottom edges of the finished project.

3. At the top edge, mark 2½″ from both sides of the pin. At the bottom edge, mark 6″ from both sides of the pin.

4. With both fabrics still layered, cut from a 2½″ mark at the top edge to a 6″ mark at the bottom edge. Repeat on the other side. You now have 1 middle and 2 sides from *each* fabric. *Fig. A*

5. Align the straight edges of 2 side pieces from the same fabric, right sides together. Stitch down the straight edge. Press the seam open. Repeat with the side pieces from the other fabric. *Figs. B–C*

6. Layer all 4 pieces, both middles and both pieced sides, and trim all edges so the 4 pieces are identical in size.

7. Align 2 shapes of the same fabric with right sides together. Sew along the short edge to create an elongated hourglass shape. Press seam open. Repeat for the other 2 shapes. *Fig. D*

8. Lay both hourglass shapes right sides together. Sew them together along both long edges, pivoting at the center seam. Leave the ends open. Turn right side out and press well. *Fig. E*

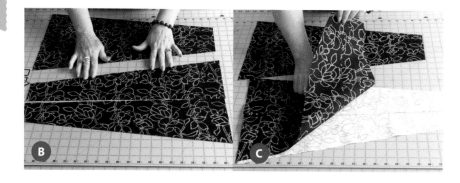

B

C

D

E

9. With the main fabric facing out, insert the fabric into your hanger (ring, handle, or tieback). Position the hanger at the center fold. *Fig. F*

10. Pin the bottom edges of the lining fabric right sides together, and continue pinning an inch or so of the main fabric together past each side seam. Sew the pinned section together. *Fig. G*

11. Remove the pins. Place the hanger in front of you with the opening on top. Lay one seam allowance of the opening flat. Fold the other seam allowance wrong sides together. Press flat. Topstitch a scant ⅛″ from the folded edge to close the opening. *Figs. H–I*

12. Topstitch around both side edges of the fabric hanger. *Fig. J*

13. For a cord tieback, twist and fold it over to form a hanging loop. *Fig. K*

F   G

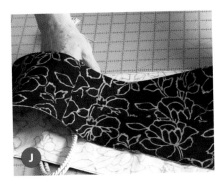

H   I

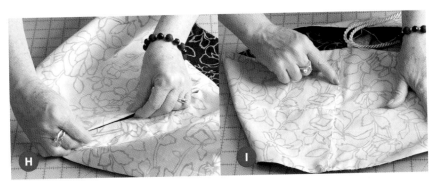

J   K

Fabric Envelope

FINISHED SIZE: 7½″ × 7½″

I started out with 11½″ fabric squares and a 10½″ interfacing square to make a 7½″ square envelope, but you can use any size of a square you like. The key is to make the interfacing square 1″ smaller than the fabric square. This is a quick and easy project you can make at any size using leftover fabric.

Use Up Scraps
Sizeable
Precut Friendly

Requirements

Main fabric: 1 square
11½″ × 11½″

Lining fabric: 1 square
11½″ × 11½″

**Midweight double-sided
fusible interfacing:**
1 square 10½″ × 10½″
(I like Structure 2 by Fairfield.)

Ribbon: 15″ length

Eyelets: 3, approximately ⅜″

Fray-stop liquid

Erasable fabric pen,
such as a FriXion pen (by Pilot)

Hammer

Construction

*All seam allowances are ¼″ unless
otherwise noted.*

1. Apply fray-stop liquid liberally
to both ends of the ribbon. Coat at
least 1″ of length at each end. When
it dries, apply a second coat. Set the
ribbon aside.

2. Mark the center of each side of the
interfacing with an erasable fabric
pen. Do not adhere it to the fabric yet.
Fig. A

3. Lay the corner of a grid ruler at a
45° angle on one center mark, aligning
the corners of 1″ with the edge of the
interfacing. Trace the triangle. Cut it
out and gently round the corners.
Repeat for all sides. *Figs. B–C*

4. Round the 4 outside corners of the
square. *Fig. D*

5. Lay both fabric squares right sides
together. Center the interfacing onto
the wrong side of the outside fabric
square. Pin the 3 layers together. *Fig. E*

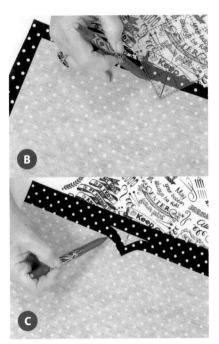

6. Sew the fabric layers together, using the edge of the interfacing as your stitch guide. Leave a 4″ opening along one side. Backstitch both ends of the opening. *Fig. F*

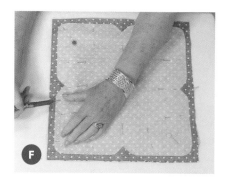

7. Snip into the center of each notch, close to the seam. Then trim and clip the seam allowance at all the curves. *Figs. G–H*

8. Fold and press the outside fabric seam allowance onto the fusible interfacing. Take care to avoid touching the interfacing with your iron. *Fig. I*

Laura's Tip

Use a kitchen fork when working closely with an iron to help avoid the heat. *Fig. J*

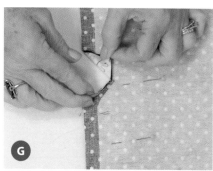
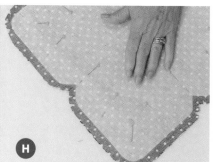

9. Turn right side out, shaping all the corners and notches. Tuck the opening seam allowance inside. Press both sides of the envelope well to fuse the fabric to the interfacing. Topstitch all around, ¼″ from the edge. *Fig. K*

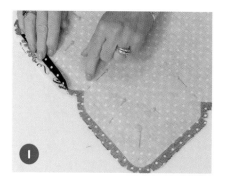
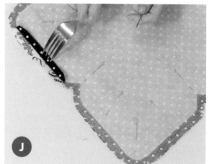

10. Fold one corner from notch to notch, lining sides together. Press along the fold. Repeat for all 4 corners. *Fig. L*

11. Trim the ends of the ribbon at an angle. Fold the ribbon in half, and center the folded end on the bottom flap point with a ½″ overlap. Sew it in place with a few backstitches. *Fig. M*

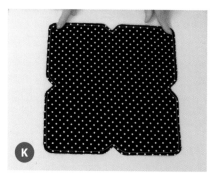

12. Following the manufacturer's instructions, install an eyelet to each of the side flaps and the top flap, centered and ½″ from the edge.

13. Thread both ribbon tails through one side eyelet and then through the other side. *Figs. N–O*

14. To close the envelope, thread one ribbon tail through the top eyelet. Tie both ribbon tails together in a bow.

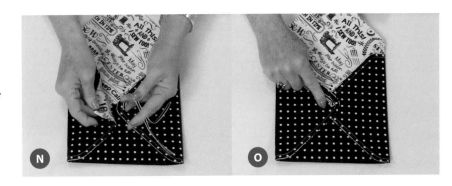

Reversible "Not Just for Clothespins" Bag

FINISHED SIZE:
Approximately 15½″ × 20″

This is such a handy storage idea, and it requires only 4 fat quarters and a hanger. Keep it in the laundry room or near the clothesline with pins. Place it in a closet with gloves and scarves. Hang it on the bathroom door to keep toiletries. Or set it next to your sewing machine to corral your scraps as you make things.

Precut Friendly

Requirements

Main fabric: 2 fat quarters

Lining fabric: 2 fat quarters

Round object (like a side plate): Approximately 7″ diameter for template

Infant-size hanger: Approximately 14″ wide

Construction

All seam allowances are ¼″ unless otherwise noted.

1. Lay 1 outside and 1 lining fat quarter right sides together, aligning all edges. Trim the edges so they are straight. Fold the top fabric in half, wrong sides together, along the 22″ length. Finger-press the fold. Unfold the fabric. *Fig. A*

2. Center the hanger at one end of the folded line, with the bottom edge perpendicular to the line. Place the bottom of the hook about 2″ below the fabric edge. *Fig. B*

3. Center the round template on the fold line, with the 7″ round template 1½″ from the bottom of the hanger (or 4½″ from the bottom of the hook). Trace the template. *Fig. C*

4. Shorten your machine stitch length and sew both layers of fabric right sides together along the traced line. Cut out the inner circle, leaving a ¼″ seam allowance. Every ¼″, clip the seam allowance close to the seam. *Figs. D–E*

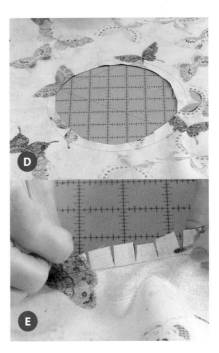

5. Insert one layer of fabric into the hole and turn it so both layers are right side out. Press. Topstitch around the circle. Consider using a decorative stitch. *Figs. F–G*

Laura's Note

If the round seam does not lie flat in a few places, reclip the seam allowance at the puckers.

6. At the top edge of both fabrics, fold the fabric ½˝ to the wrong side. Along a 5˝ section at the center, topstitch the fabrics together ⅛˝ from the folds. *Fig. H*

7. To make the back, stitch the remaining 2 fat quarters together along an 18˝ edge, right sides together. Fold them wrong sides together and press the seam.

8. Lay the bag front on top of the back, right sides together and align the top edges.

9. Fold the front layer in half. Finger-press the center fold at the top edge. Unfold the top layer. *Fig. I*

10. Align the bottom of the hanger hook with the center fold along the top folded edge and trace the hanger shoulders. *Fig. J*

11. Working with all the layers together, trim both sides 4½˝ from the outside edge of the circle.

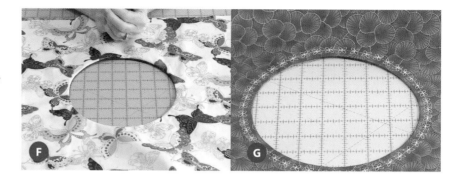

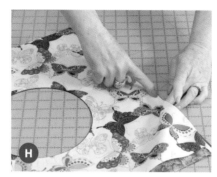

Topstitch 5˝ along top edge.

Finger-press fold above circle.

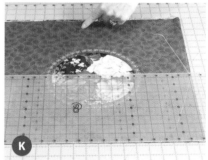

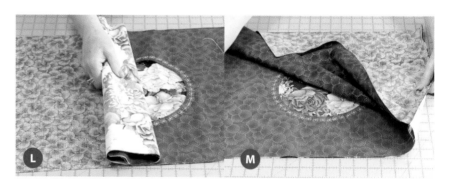

Then trim 8˝ from the bottom edge of the circle. The bag should measure approximately 16½˝ × 20½˝. *Fig. K*

12. Ensure the layers are oriented right sides together. Hold the top 3 layers with one hand and bring the bottom layer up and around to the top, folding it over the top 3 layers so the lining fabrics are now right sides together. *Figs. L–M*

13. Mark the center of the top seam with a pin. Center the hanger on the lining at the pin, with the bottom of the hook at the stitched seam. Trace the hanger on the wrong side of the lining. Retrace the line with a ruler to the side edges, leaving a 1″ space along the top seam for the hook. *Figs. N–O*

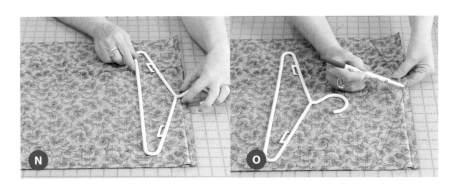

14. Pin all layers together along the hanger lines and down the sides, leaving the bottom 3″ unpinned. Fold the top lining layer wrong sides together along the 3″ mark and pin the flap in place. Pin and sew the 3 remaining bottom layers together along the bottom seam. *Fig. P*

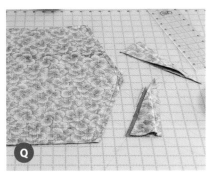

15. Unfold the top layer, align all the bottom edges, and pin the remaining sections of the side seams together. Starting at the 1″ space along the top edge, sew along the traced line and down the side to the bottom edge. Backstitch both ends of each seam. Trim the shoulders, leaving a ¼″ seam allowance. Repeat on the other side. *Fig. Q*

16. Turn the bag so the lining is right side out. Tuck under a ¼″ seam allowance at the bottom edge, press, and whipstitch the bottom edge closed. *Fig. R*

17. The bag is now finished in the "reversed" position. Insert the hanger now or turn the bag "right side" out and insert hanger.

Needlebooks

FINISHED SIZE: Approximately 2½˝ × 2½˝

These sweet little booklets are the perfect thing to keep your sewing needles stored and organized. They're great for traveling, and they also fit inside a wallet as an emergency sewing kit. They are a terrific gift idea for all your stitch-y friends.

This pattern yields 2 needlebooks, each with 4 pages.

Use Up Scraps
Precut Friendly

Requirements

These materials are enough for 2 needlebooks.

Main fabric: 1 square 5″ × 5″

Inside fabric: 1 square 5″ × 5″

Flannel or felt: 2 squares 5″ × 5″ for pages

Lightweight double-sided fusible web: 1 square 5″ × 5″ (I like Stick by Fairfield.)

Pinking shears or pinking rotary blade

Laura's Tip

If you want to make a large batch of needlebooks for a guild or for your sewing friends, you can use 2 fabric fat quarters, 1 fusible fleece fat quarter, and 1 flannel fat quarter to yield 24 notebooks with 2 pages each!

Construction

All seam allowances are ¼″ unless otherwise noted.

1. Fuse both fabrics together, right sides out, with the fusible web between them.

2. Cut the fused square in half to make 2 rectangles 2½″ × 5″. Trim all edges with pinking shears. These are the book covers.

3. Cut 4 flannel rectangles 2″ × 4½″ with pinking shears. Layer 2 flannel pages, centered, onto the inside cover of each book. *Fig. A*

4. Starting at the center of the top edge of the book, sew down the middle of all 3 layers to secure the pages in place. Stop sewing with the needle down ⅛″ from the bottom edge. Pivot and topstitch ⅛″ from the edge all around, pivoting at all 4 corners. Move the flannel pages out of the way if necessary. *Figs. B–C*

When you return to the first pivot point, pivot again to complete the middle seam to the bottom edge of the book. *Fig. D*

5. Fold the book in half with the cover on the outside. Create a spine by sewing a seam ⅛″ from the folded edge, backstitching at both ends of the seam. *Fig. E*

A

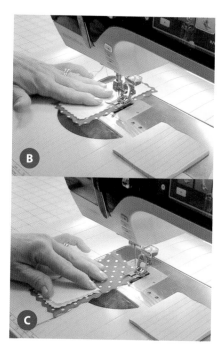

B

C

D

E

Cathedral Window Pincushion

FINISHED SIZE: 5½″ × 5½″

If you don't like hand sewing, you will love this project! Only the little button needs a few hand stitches. Think of all the fabric combinations you could use for this handy little sewing notion.

Use Up Scraps

Requirements

Main fabric: 1 square 8½″ × 8½″

Trim fabric: 1 square 8½″ × 8½″

Inside fabric: 1 square 6″ × 6″

Shank button

Basting glue

Fabric pen

Polyester stuffing

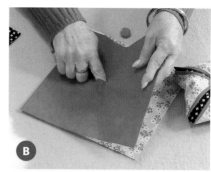

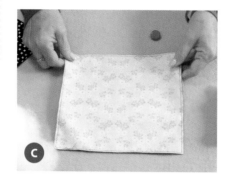

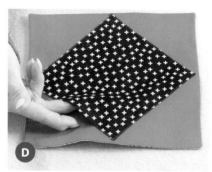

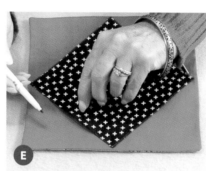

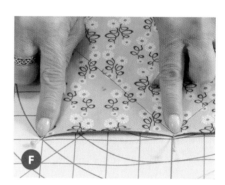

Construction

All seam allowances are ¼″ unless otherwise noted.

1. Press a ¼″ seam allowance to the wrong side along all 4 edges of the inside fabric. Glue baste the folds in place. *Fig. A*

2. Snip a little hole in the center of the trim fabric. *Fig. B*

3. Reduce the stitch length on your sewing machine. Right sides together, sew the trim and main fabric squares together along all 4 edges. (Start sewing about 1″ from a corner, not at a corner.) Trim the seam allowance to ⅛″. *Fig. C*

4. Turn the cushion right side out through the snipped hole. Enlarge the hole slightly if necessary. Shape the corners. Press the edges well.

5. Center the inside square on the trim fabric side of the cushion, ensuring the corners of the inside fabric meet the center points of each edge exactly. Pin the corners in place. Sew the layers together ⅛″ from the edge of the inside fabric square, leaving a 2″ opening along one edge. *Fig. D*

6. Trace along the fold at the opening with a fabric pen. It will not be visible when the cushion is done. *Fig. E*

7. On an ironing surface, place the trim side down. Pin at each corner and at the center of each side. *Fig. F*

Apply a small bead of glue on the main fabric close to the edge between 2 pins. *Fig. G*

Fold both layers to the main fabric, exposing the trim, and press. Glue and press the fold in place. *Fig. H*

Repeat for all 8 segments. Press well.

8. Working one side of the square at a time, start at a corner and sew the folds in place, stitching close to the inside curved edge. Stop at the next corner. Leave 10″ thread tails at both ends of each seam. You should have 4 thread tails at each corner. Repeat for all sides. Press well. *Fig. I*

9. Insert stuffing under the inside fabric, ensuring the corners are filled. Pin and sew the opening closed along the drawn line with the sewing machine. *Figs. J–K*

10. Fold 2 opposite corners onto the inside fabric and tie the tails together, ensuring the corner points meet in the middle. Use pins to hold the corners in place while you tie the threads if necessary. Repeat with the remaining corners. *Figs. L–M*

11. Group the tails into 2 sections. Thread one section through a large-eyed needle. Thread the needle through the button shank, then insert the needle through the entire cushion at the center. *Fig. N*

On the bottom side, insert the needle close to the first hole and pull the needle back to the top of the cushion. *Fig. O*

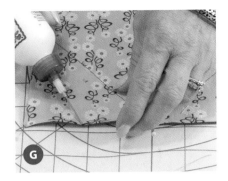

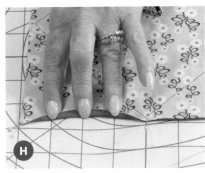

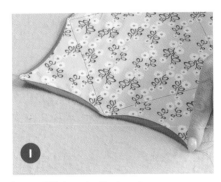

Leave 10″ thread tails at each corner.

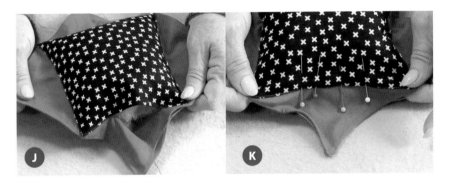

Remove the needle from the threads. Tug the threads gently to secure the button and make a dimple. Using both sets of tails, tie the threads together with a few knots. *Figs. P–Q*

Wrap one set of tails around the button tightly and tie another 2 knots. Trim the thread tails under the button. *Figs. R–S*

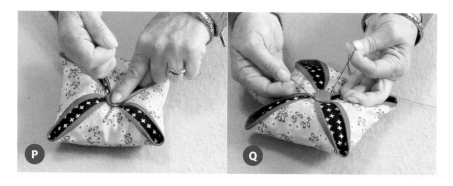

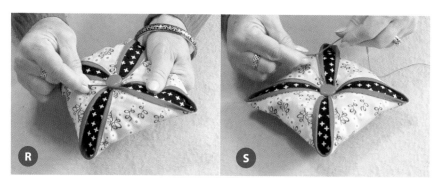

Quilt Block Rollup

FINISHED SIZE: Approximately 18″ × 36″ when opened

Once you've cut and pressed your quilt block pieces, or prepared all your appliqué shapes, you don't want them to get all wrinkled or disorganized or—heaven forbid—lost! This organizer has two large "pages" of batting and a zippered pocket to help you keep all your pieces together in one tidy place.

Requirements

Main fabric: 1 strip 20″ × width of fabric

Contrast fabric: 2 circles 3½″ diameter

Fleece: 2 rectangles 17″ × 24″

Cording or ribbon: 1¼ yards

7″ zipper

Pipe insulation, ½″ diameter (inside hole): 18″ length

Wooden dowel, ¾″ diameter: 18″ length

Craft glue

Elastic bands: 2

Construction

All seam allowances are ¼″ unless otherwise noted.

1. Insert the dowel into the insulation sleeve to form a padded roll.

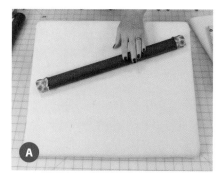

2. Apply craft glue to the wrong side of one fabric circle. Center it to one end of the roll and fold the edges of the circle onto the sides of the padded roll. Secure the circle with an elastic band and let the glue dry. Repeat with the other end of the roll. *Fig. A*

Caution: Do not use a glue gun—hot glue will melt the pipe insulation foam.

3. Trim the selvages from the main fabric. On each side, fold the fabric to the wrong side ½″; then fold again ½″ to create a double-fold ½″ hem. Press and sew close to the inside folded edge. Repeat for the other long edge. The hemmed panel should be the same width as the padded roll. *Fig. B*

4. At one end of the fabric panel, fold ½″ to the wrong side. Press and stitch along the raw edge to secure the fold. *Fig. C*

5. Fold and pin the unfinished end of the panel right sides together, aligning the hemmed side edges. *Fig. D*

6. Lay the zipper centered between the folded edge and the hemmed edges. Mark the exact length of the teeth—ignore the extra tape on both ends. It should be 7″. On the back of the fabric at both ends of the zipper, mark a ½″ seam allowance from the end of the zipper teeth. This will leave approximately 1″ on each end, depending on the width of your hemmed panel. *Fig. E*

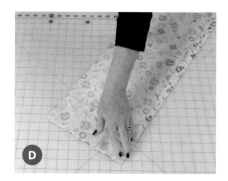

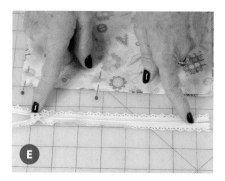

Sew the 2 ends closed. You will have the opening for the zipper still open. *Fig. F*

7. Clip the seam allowance at the folded edge. *Fig. G*

8. Press the seam open, including the space left for the zipper. *Fig. H*

9. Turn the folded corner right side out. Trim the ends of the zipper, leaving ½˝ at both ends. Align the teeth with the fold of the seam, and pin in place. To install a decorative zipper, center it faceup on top of the right side of the open seam. To install a standard zipper, place it faceup on the wrong side of the open seam. *Figs. I–J*

10. Sew around the zipper approximately ¼˝ from the teeth. *Figs. K–L*

11. Align the zipper seam with the center of the hemmed panel. Topstitch across the hemmed edge of the corner, ¼˝ from the edge, to create a pocket. *Fig. M*

12. Fold the cord or ribbon in half. Pin and sew to the non-zipper side of the point. Knot and fray the ends. *Fig. N*

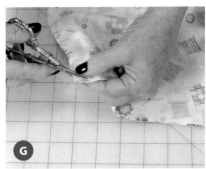

Decorative zipper placement   Standard zipper placement

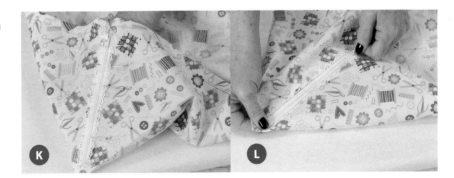

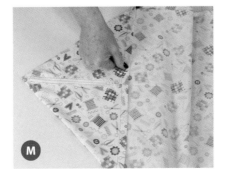

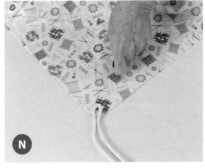

13. On the short hemmed edge, measure and fold 3½″ from the hemmed edge. Press. *Fig. O*

14. Measure 2½″ from that fold, draw a line, and sew along that line. *Fig. P*

15. Lay 2 batting pieces on the wrong side of the hemmed panel, tucking the short edges under the 1″ flap from Step 14. Topstitch through all layers along the folded edge of the flap. *Figs. Q–R*

16. Remove the elastic bands from the padded roll ends and insert it into the 2½″ casing from Step 14. *Optional:* Glue the wrong side of the casing hem to the sides of the roll. *Figs. S–T*

17. Smooth the layers of batting along the wrong side of the panel. Roll up the roll along the batting, smoothing the batting again as needed. Trim the batting corners approximately 1″ from the edge of the fabric. *Fig. U*

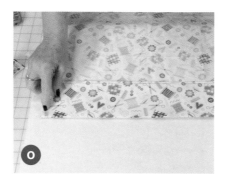

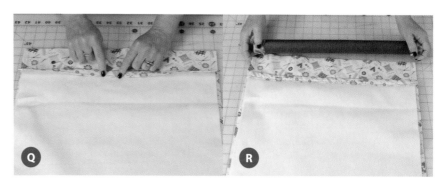

Sewing Armchair Caddy

This is a handy accessory if you love to stitch while you're sitting on a couch or a nice big armchair. This caddy has six pockets, thread and scissor holders, and a nice big pincushion so nothing will get lost in or under the furniture.

Use Up Scraps
Sizeable

Requirements

Foam or quilt batting:
1 rectangle 10″ × 21″

Back fabric: 1 rectangle
10″ × 21″

Front fabric: 1 rectangle
10″ × 11″ and 1 rectangle
10″ × 17″

Large pocket: 1 rectangle
10″ × 13½″

Medium pocket: 1 rectangle
10″ × 11″

Small pocket: 1 rectangle
10″ × 8″

Binding: 2 strips 2½″ × width
of fabric

⅛″-wide ribbon: 3 yards

**Thin, strong plastic straw
(like a coffee stir stick):**
Small enough to fit through a
spool

Erasable fabric pen, such as
a FriXion pen (by Pilot)

Fabric glue

**Polyester stuffing and
crushed walnut shells**
for pincushion

Construction

*All seam allowances are ¼″ unless
otherwise noted.*

1. Fold and press each pocket
rectangle in half, wrong sides
together, to measure 10″ wide. Draw
a line down the center of the right
side of the small pocket. Draw 2 lines
down the right side of the medium
pocket, each 3½″ from the side edges.
Fig. A

2. Lay the small pocket onto the
medium pocket, right sides up, and
align the bottom and side raw edges.
Pin the layers together and stitch
along the centerline on the small
pocket, backstitching the seam at the
fold. *Fig. B*

3. Cut 3 lengths of ribbon: 14″, 15″,
and 16″ for the spool holders. Cut
3 segments from the straw, 1½″ each.
Thread a straw segment onto each
ribbon. Cut a 1½-yard length of
ribbon for the scissor keep. *Fig. C*

4. Fold all 3 spool ribbons and the
scissor-keep ribbon in half. Pin and
baste the raw edges along a 10″ edge
of the 10″ × 11″ front fabric. *Fig. D*

5. Lay both front pieces right sides
together, aligning the basted ribbon
edge with a 10″ edge of the 10″ × 17″
piece. Sew the layers together along
the ribbon-basted edge. *Fig. E*

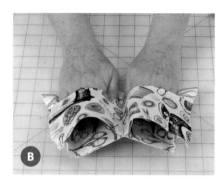

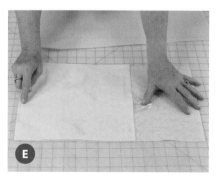

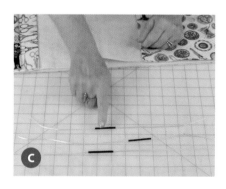

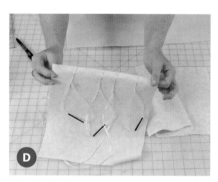

Sew front pieces together along
ribbon-basted edge.

6. Apply fabric glue to one side of the foam. Lay the back fabric onto the glued side of the foam, wrong sides together. Press to set the glue. *Fig. F*

7. Lay the pieced front onto the unglued side of the foam, wrong sides together, aligning the 10″ end of the ribbon section to one end. *Fig. G*

Fold the 17″ front piece back onto the 11″ front piece, right sides together, exposing the seam. Sew through all layers along the pieced seam. *Fig. H*

8. Align the end of the 17″ top piece to the other end of the foam. Smooth the fabric over the ribbons, ensuring that the ribbons are lying flat. Pin the fold and corners in place. *Figs. I–J*

9. Turn the piece over so the back side is facing up. Sew through all layers right along the stitched line from Step 7. *Fig. K*

10. With the front side up, align the center of the folded section with the seam underneath. Pin the edges in place. *Fig. L*

11. Pin the small/medium pockets to the 11″ side of the caddy, aligning the bottom edges. Fold the small pocket to one side, exposing a drawn line on the medium pocket. Stitch along the line on the medium pocket, backstitching the top of the seam at the fold. Repeat to stitch the other line on the medium pocket. *Figs. M–N*

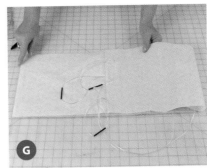

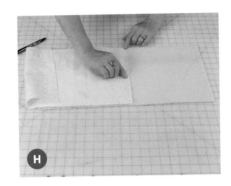

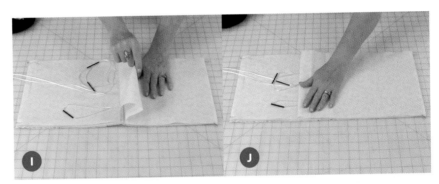

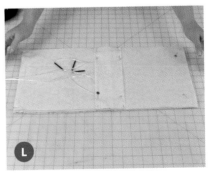

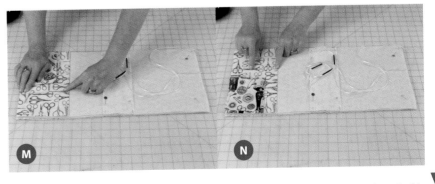

12. Pin and baste the raw edges of the small/medium pockets to the foam. *Fig. O*

13. Pin and baste the large pocket to the other end of the foam, aligning the raw edges. *Fig. P*

14. Sew a scant ¼″ from the edge to close one end of the pincushion fold. *Fig. Q*

Fill the fold approximately one-third full with stuffing. Fill the next third with crushed walnut shells. Fill the rest with stuffing. Do not overfill the pincushion. Pin and sew the remaining opening closed with a scant ¼″ seam. *Fig. R*

15. Shift the stuffing on both sides of the pincushion away from the edges and pin the outer edge seam allowances flat. *Fig. S*

16. Piece the 2½″ × width of fabric strips together and trim to approximately 2½″ × 68″. Fold and press the strip in half lengthwise, wrong sides together. Lay the binding along one edge right sides together, aligning raw edges. Leaving a 4″ tail, sew a ¼″ seam. Stop ¼″ from the corner and sew a few reverse stitches. *Fig. T*

Fold the binding away from the caddy. Then fold it down along the next edge, aligning the raw edges. Sew from the top edge down the caddy. Repeat on each corner. *Figs. U–V*

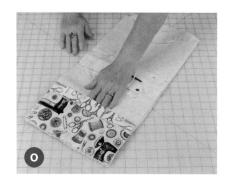

O

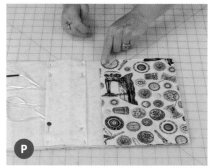

P

Q

R

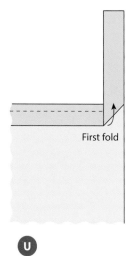

S

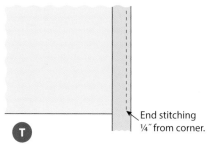

End stitching ¼″ from corner.

T

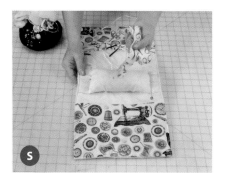

First fold

U

Second fold

V

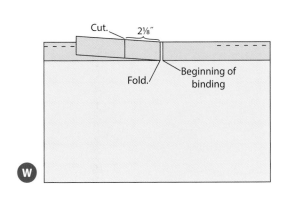

Cut. 2⅛″

Fold.

Beginning of binding

W

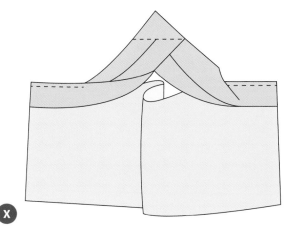

X

Stop sewing 5″ from the starting point. Overlap the end by 2½″. Trim the excess length. Open the fold at both ends. Align the ends as shown, right sides together. Pin and sew them together. Trim the excess, leaving a ¼″ seam allowance. *Figs. W–X*

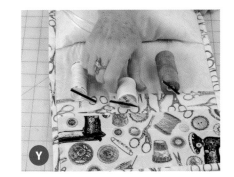

Y

Press the seam open and refold/press binding. Then finish sewing the binding to the caddy. Fold the binding over the raw caddy edges onto the back. Hand stitch the folded binding edge to the caddy back with an invisible stitch.

17. To keep a spool, thread one end of a straw through the spool hole and out the other side. Position the straw like a toggle at the bottom of the spool. *Fig. Y*

18. To keep a pair of scissors, insert the folded end of the ribbon through one handle. Then insert the scissors through the loop and pull the ribbon snugly. *Figs. Z–Z²*

Z

Z¹

Z²

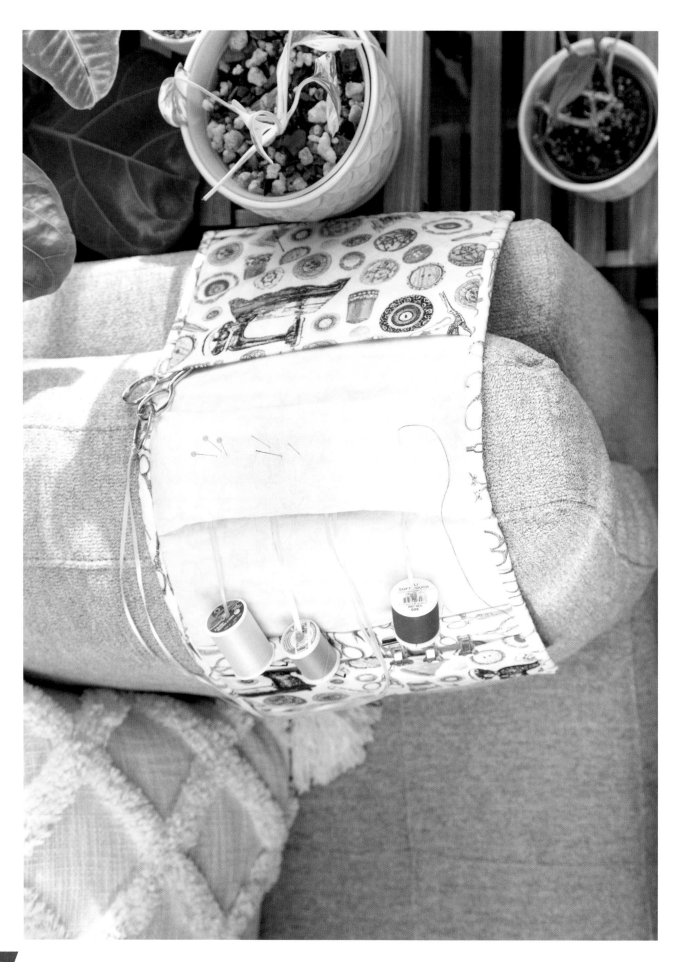

Custom Featherweight Case Cover

Featherweight cases are very old and very valuable, so it's best to keep them protected from unnecessary wear and tear. This padded cover will do the job nicely, and you get to choose the perfect fabrics for your cover.

Sizeable

Requirements

Main fabric: ½ yard

Bottom fabric: ½ yard

Trim fabric: ½ yard

Lining fabric: 1 yard

Double-sided fusible foam stabilizer: Approximately 30″ × 50″ (I like In-R-Form Plus by Bosal.)

18″ non-separating zippers: 2

Flexible measuring tape

Erasable fabric pen, such as a FriXion pen (by Pilot)

Construction

All seam allowances are ¼″ unless otherwise noted.

1. Measure around the sides of the case at the clasps. Add 2″ to that measurement. This is your *width* measurement. Fig. A

Measure around the height of the case at the handle. Add 2″ to that measurement and divide the number by 2. This is your *height* measurement. Fig. B

2. Cut a foam rectangle to equal the width × height.

3. Cut a lining rectangle to match the foam, plus 2″ to each dimension for quilting ease.

4. Cut the cover fabrics to these measurements:

- **Main fabric:** A rectangle to equal the foam width × 12½″

- **Trim fabric:** A rectangle to equal the foam width × 3½″

- **Bottom fabric:** A rectangle to equal the foam width × 9½″

Laura's Note

If your main or lining fabric is not wide enough, cut 2 extra strips from the trim fabric 3½″ × the height.

5. Piece the main, trim, and bottom fabrics together and press the seams open. If necessary, sew the 3½″ trim strips to the sides of the pieced panel. Fig. C

6. Center and fuse the foam to the wrong sides of the lining. Then lay the pieced cover, right side up, on the other side of the foam, aligning the top edge of the main fabric with the top edge of the foam. *Fig. D*

7. Quilt as desired. Trim excess fabric. *Fig. E*

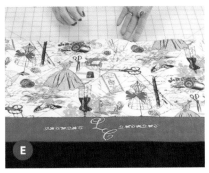

8. Measure the case from the center of the lid to the bottom of the clasp plate. *Fig. F*

Mark that distance from the top edge of the quilted panel. Draw a horizontal line across the panel width and cut the panel along that line. *Figs. G–H*

9. Mark the center of the cut line. Open a zipper and mark ½″ from the top end of the zipper. *Fig. I*

With right sides together, lay one-half of the zipper on the top section, aligning the center mark on the panel with the ½″ mark on the zipper. Pin the zipper along the edge. With a zipper attachment, sew the zipper to the top panel. *Fig. J*

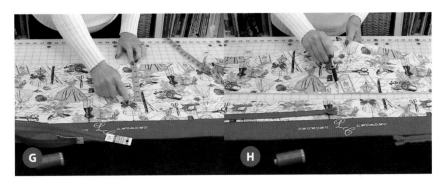

Repeat to lay half of the other zipper on the remaining edge of the top panel, overlapping the zipper tops by ½″. *Fig. K*

Sew half of the second zipper to the panel. *Fig. L*

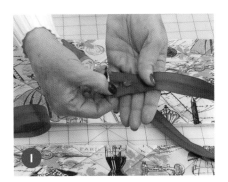
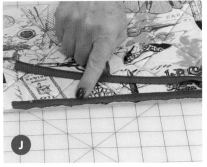

10. Repeat Step 9 to sew the zippers to the bottom panel. *Fig. M*

11. Topstitch both zipper seam allowances flat, stopping where the teeth end at the bottom of the zipper. *Fig. N*

12. To join the remainder of the panels together, snip the seam allowance at the end of the topstitching. *Fig. O*

With the cover laying right side up, smooth the section at the end of the zipper. If the fabric overlaps, trace the edge of the top layer and trim it off. *Figs. P–R*

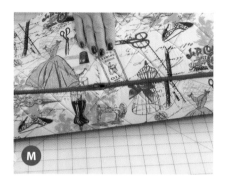

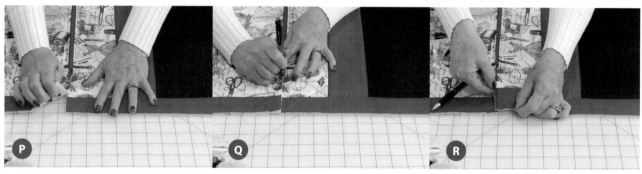

Overlapping edges

Trace overlap.

Trim overlap.

Sew the rest of the seam together with a zigzag stitch. *Fig. S*

To cover the zigzag stitches, cut a piece of trim fabric 2½″ × (length of seam + ¼″). Fold and press over ¼″ at one short end. Then fold and press both raw edges wrong sides together to meet in the middle. *Fig. T*

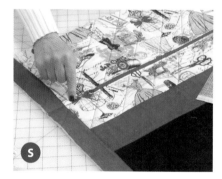
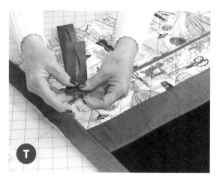

Lay the pressed trim, right side up, over the zigzag stitches, aligning the short, folded end with the end of the zipper. Topstitch along the 3 pressed edges. Trim the excess. Repeat on the other side. *Fig. U*

13. Test the fit of the quilted panel around the sides of your case. Trim if necessary and sew the sides right sides together with a ½″ seam. *Fig. V*

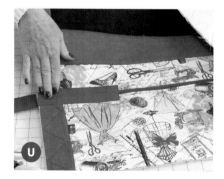

14. To bind the top edge, cut a strip of bottom fabric 2½″ × the top edge length, plus a few extra inches. Piece if necessary. Fold the strip lengthwise, wrong sides together, and press. Then fold one short end ½″, wrong sides together, and press. Pin the binding to the top edge of the cover, aligning the raw edges. Overlap the binding end by ½″ and trim the excess. Tuck the raw edge inside the folded edge, and pin. Sew the binding to the cover with a ¼″ seam. *Fig. W*

Fold the binding over the raw edges. Pin the binding to the lining and sew it in place. *Fig. X*

15. With the quilted cover inside out, fold the bottom edge up, wrong sides together, to meet the zipper. Fit the sleeve over the case, aligning the back seam with the center back of the case. *Fig. Y*

Fold the bound edges to meet the handle at the top as shown. Fold the corners toward the top and mark the flaps with pins along the side edges of the case. *Fig. Z*

Remove the cover and sew along both rows of pins. *Fig. A¹*

Turn right side out. Align the binding on the corner flaps with the binding along the opening and hand stitch in place. *Fig. B¹*

16. Open the zippers, turn the cover inside out again, and fit it over the case. Turn the case upside down. *Fig. C¹*

Taking care to not pull too hard (the zipper is slightly open), fold the bottom edges to meet in the middle. Pin the foam along the center to mark the seam. *Fig. D¹*

Remove the case. Fold the cover in half with the back seam in the middle, and sew the bottom seam marked with pins.

With the quilted cover still inside out, insert the case again, fitting the bottoms. *Fig. E¹*

17. Fold the corners toward the bottom and mark the flaps with pins along the side edges of the case. *Fig. F¹*

Remove the cover. Fold the bottom seam open and sew along both rows of pins. Trim the corner, leaving a ¼˝ seam allowance. Zigzag the raw edges. *Figs. G¹–H¹*

18. Turn the cover right side out and shape the corners.

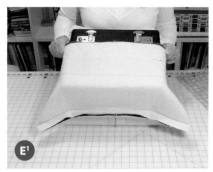

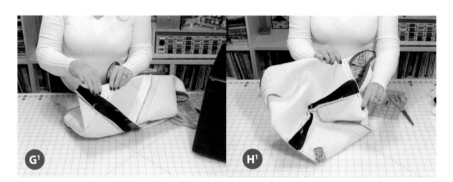

Custom Sewing Machine Cover

It is so important to cover our sewing machines when they are not in use to protect them from all the dust we generate with our fabric and thread, along with regular household dust. A cover is so simple to make, and you can customize it to fit your machine exactly.

Sizeable

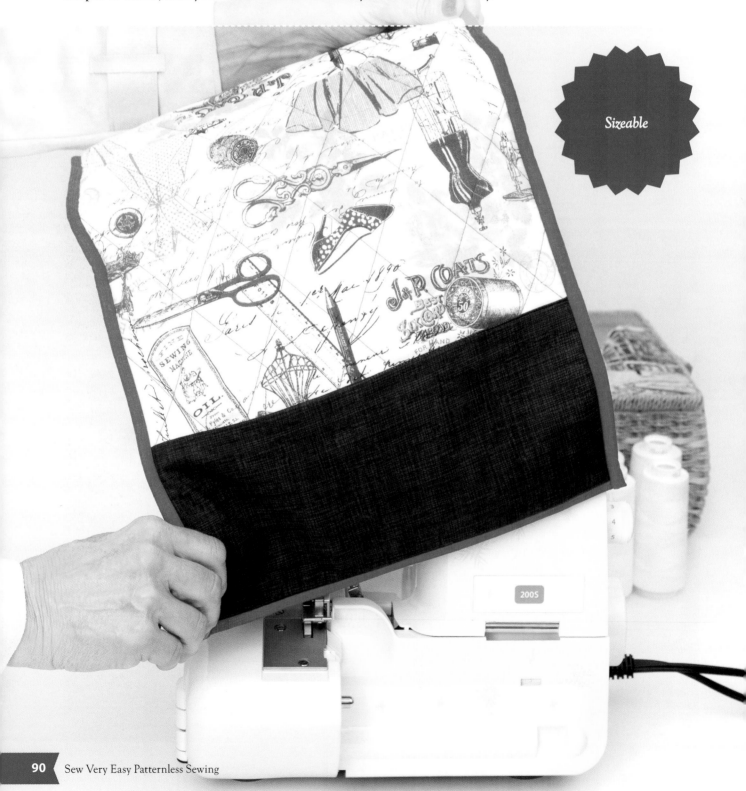

Requirements

This pattern is designed for you to custom-fit your machine, so fabric requirements listed are estimates only.

Main fabric: ½ yard

Trim fabric: ½ yard

Border fabric: ½ yard

Lining fabric: 1 yard

Foam stabilizer: ¾ yard (I like Support by Fairfield.)

Felt marker, such as a permanent marker

Cardboard: 12˝ square for template

Quilting ruler

Flexible measuring tape

Laura's Note

Before you measure your machine:

- *Decide if you want the cover to fit the machine threaded or unthreaded; install or remove the spool accordingly.*

- *Decide if you want the cover to fit the machine with the arm down or up, and position it accordingly.*

Construction

All seam allowances are ¼˝ unless otherwise noted.

1. Place the cardboard against the wheel side of your machine. With a level ruler across the top of the sewing machine, mark the height on the cardboard. Move the ruler down the front and back of the machine to mark the outline shape. *Figs. A–B*

Add 1˝ to each line. Cut out the *side* template, gently rounding the corners (excluding the bottom). Double-check the size against the machine, and adjust if necessary. *Fig. C*

2. Measure the *width* of your machine and add 2˝ to that dimension. *Fig. D*

3. With a measuring tape, measure around the template edge, excluding the bottom side. This measurement is the *cover* length. Label the sides on your template. Also note the cover *length* and *width* dimensions on the template. *Fig. E*

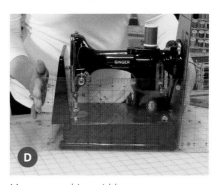

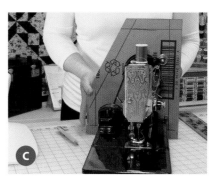

Measure machine width.

4. Trace and cut out 2 foam sides. *Fig. F*

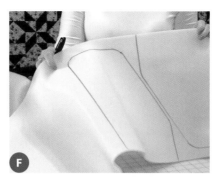

5. Using the *cover length* and *width* dimensions, cut out a foam rectangle. *Fig. G*

6. Cut the following fabrics:

Laura's Tip

Customize the fabric placement as desired. The measurements below are to create the original design shown in the photos.

Main fabric:

- 1 rectangle the *cover width* × the *cover length*. Subtract the border height from the cover length if necessary.

- 2 rectangles 7″ × the *side width*

Border fabric:

- 2 borders 5″ × the *cover length*

- 2 borders 5″ × the *side width*

Trim fabric:

- 1 strip 3″ × the *cover width* (optional)

- 3 strips 2″ × the width of fabric

- 2 strips 2″ × (the *cover length* + 3″)

7. Sew a cover-length border to each short end of the main fabric. Press. *Fig. H*

8. Center and fuse the foam to the wrong sides of the lining. Then lay the pieced cover, right side up, on the other side of the foam. Quilt all 3 layers as desired. Trim the excess fabric and zigzag the edges. *Fig. I*

9. Fuse the foam sides to the side lining pieces, and add the side main fabric to the top of each piece of foam. Ensure you have a right-facing side and a left-facing side. Quilt if desired and zigzag the edges. *Fig. J*

10. Add a decorative trim if desired. *Fig. K*

11. Binding: Fold and press a 2″ trim fabric strip in half lengthwise, wrong sides together. Cut 2 lengths that are the *side width* and 2 lengths that are the *cover width*. Aligning the raw edges, sew one binding strip to the bottom edge of a side piece, right sides together. *Fig. L*

Fold the binding over the raw edges and sew it to the lining by hand or machine. *Fig. M*

Repeat to bind the remaining 3 bottom edges. *Fig. N*

12. Sew each 2″ × (the *cover length* + 3″) binding strip to a long edge of the cover, right sides together, leaving 1½″ tails at each end. Do not fold the strips over the raw edges—leave them flat against the cover. *Fig. O*

13. Pin the back edge of each side to the cover, wrong sides together, aligning the bottom edges. Wrap the binding tails around the bottom edges and pin in place. *Fig. P*

Sew both sides to the cover, just along the back edges of the side pieces. *Fig. Q*

14. Pin the front edge of the sides to the cover, wrong sides together, aligning the bottom edges. Wrap the binding tails around the bottom edges and pin in place. Sew both sides to the cover, just along the bottom 4″ of the side pieces. *Fig. R*

15. Pin and sew the remaining sections of each side to the cover, easing as necessary. *Fig. S*

16. Hand stitch the folded edge of the binding to the sides. *Fig. T*

About the Author

Laura Coia is the founder and celebrity host of the very successful and inspiring SewVeryEasy YouTube channel, founded in 2014. In addition to representing Quilt Canada, she has been awarded the Silver Creator Award by YouTube and an Ultimate Zoomer Award by ZoomerMedia Limited.

Laura is a freelance seamstress, educator, and registered professional with more than 45 years of experience in teaching quilting, tailoring, garment repairs, and garment construction. She teaches all aspects of sewing and quilting while motivating people to spend quality time in the sewing room. Laura has developed and shared many tips, techniques, and new ideas for the novice as well as the experienced sewist. Her videos and instructions are easy to follow, inspiring students to get their projects done.

Laura is also a published pattern designer and book author. She has written for various sewing and quilting magazines, holds seminars and workshops, and does trunk shows as well as speaking engagements.

Laura's greatest joy is helping and encouraging others to enjoy what our foremothers have enjoyed for many, many years: sewing and quilting. She wants her students to take pride in their work—whether it's perfect or not—and to let their creations bring them and those around them joy and happiness.

If you watch her videos, you will see her relaxed "it's all good" approach to quilting and sewing.

Photo by Ivo Coia

Follow Laura on social media!

YouTube: /sewveryeasy

(Be sure to check out the corresponding video tutorials for each project in the book!)

Facebook: /sewveryeasy

Also by Laura Coia:

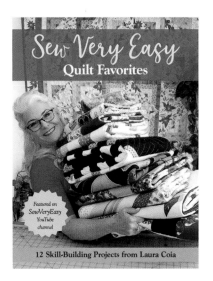